Drinking
and Dating

P.S. SOCIAL MEDIA IS RUINING ROMANCE

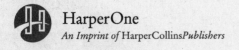

HarperOne
An Imprint of HarperCollins*Publishers*

Drinking
and
Dating

BRANDI GLANVILLE

with Leslie Bruce

HarperOne

DRINKING AND DATING: *P.S. Social Media Is Ruining Romance*. Copyright © 2014 by Brandi Glanville. All rights reserved. Printed in the United States of America. No part of this book may be used or reproduced in any manner whatsoever without written permission except in the case of brief quotations embodied in critical articles and reviews. For information address HarperCollins Publishers, 195 Broadway, New York, NY 10007.

HarperCollins books may be purchased for educational, business, or sales promotional use. For information please e-mail the Special Markets Department at SPsales@harpercollins.com.

HarperCollins website: http://www.harpercollins.com

HarperCollins®, ®, and HarperOne™ are trademarks of Harper-Collins Publishers.

FIRST HARPERCOLLINS PAPERBACK EDITION PUBLISHED IN 2015

Designed by Janet M. Evans

Library of Congress Cataloging-in-Publication Data is available upon request.

ISBN 978–0–06–229716–7

15 16 17 18 19 RRD(H) 10 9 8 7 6 5 4 3 2 1

*I dedicate this book to all the men I've loved before
and to all of the single people looking for love
in this world: keep hope alive, learn from
my mistakes, and by all means #KeepItSexy.*

CONTENTS

Introduction
How to Get Screwed

Fuck me.

Since I announced this follow-up book to *Drinking and Tweeting*, I've been asked countless times to describe what my second book will be about. I'm sure people have wondered what I could possibly have left to discuss after I freely aired *all* of the dirty laundry in my first book, from my husband's torrid affairs with cocktail waitresses, well-known actresses (#MyLipsAreSealed), and one *cunt*-ry music singer to my undergoing vaginal reconstructive surgery to make my kitty seventeen again. The answer was simple: drinking, dating, and occasionally medicating . . . and other ways I've gotten fucked.

There are a million ways to get screwed in this town—and I've experienced most of them.

Learning that some douche bag, wannabe talk-show host that I went on *one* pity date with was selling completely false stories about me because not only was his career in the shitter, but I also refused to have sex with him, is one way. Getting pinned to the hood of a professional athlete's Porsche on a dark side street in Beverly Hills because neither of us could wait the fifteen-minute drive to his house is another.

I've never seemed to have a problem getting fucked—good or bad.

Now, don't go all reality-TV crazy on me and pretend to be offended. Whether you're actually saying it or just thinking it, we've all been there, and it's not just a Hollywood problem. In today's world, you don't have to be in the spotlight to get screwed. Perhaps one night you have a few too many drinks at dinner and your friend posts a drunk-eyed photo of you on Twitter or Instagram, and all of a sudden all of your "followers"—including work colleagues and family—know you're a total lightweight. Some might even say that they're really "worried about you"—which happens to be one of the most judgmental, condescending phrases ever, in my opinion. Or you're recently single and need to feel wanted and sexy again, so you call your ex-boyfriend in hopes that he'll drive out to wherever to help "Stella get her groove back" only to realize that he's been constantly following you on social media for a month and demands answers to every single post you've written since you broke up with him—all the while pretending his "friends" sent him the posts and he doesn't *actually* care.

It's been five years now since my life was forever changed. It's been five years since I discovered my ex-husband was sleeping with half of the women in Hollywood and that everything I wanted to believe with absolute certainty about my life was so very wrong. I've been separated and then divorced for almost as long as I was married, which is a strange thing to even write. Sometimes it feels like just yesterday that my ex and my baby boys were snuggling on the couch with me in our gorgeous Calabasas home. Other times it feels like it was all a crazy dream I had one night a very long time ago. But I have three permanent reminders of my marriage that I live with every day: Mason, Jake, and HPV. My boys are the light of my life. Even if on my wedding day someone had a crystal ball revealing my future heartbreak and devastating divorce, I still would have walked down that aisle. These little fuckers were and always will be worth it.

My HPV, on the other hand, was not. Statistics don't lie. Half of all sexually active Americans have HPV, although most don't even know it. #SeeYourDoctor. By age fifty, 80 percent of all American women have contracted the virus, according to various reports. It's nice to know I'm not alone, but it still doesn't make getting my cervix scraped every three months any more fun. Reading stories online where people bash you for openly talking about having contracted the virus because you were foolish enough to believe your husband was faithful also isn't my idea of a good time.

I went through hell and back, but I'm here, I'm breathing, and I'm still using wildly inappropriate language at the worst possible moments. #BrandiBlunders. I've embraced being a single mom and created a very happy life for my boys and me. I continue to make embarrassing mistakes all the time and I still have a really poor knowledge of historical political figures, but I've always owned it. #Duh. No more ex-husband to blame, no more horrible friends to make me feel bad, and no more seventeen-year-old vagina. (See chapter 4 where I discuss one of the gorgeously well-endowed men I dated. My kitty's probably more like twenty-three now, which isn't horrible. #CouldBeWorse.)

And even when I am having the worst of days—like discovering that there were photos splashed everywhere of my black thong hanging out of my cream-colored dress because I had a few too many glasses of wine while out with friends and didn't anticipate a sea of paparazzi—I still wouldn't trade my life for anything. (Side note: That also happens to be the dress I wore on the cover of my first book. Thanks, Alice + Olivia, for helping me with both the best and worst photo ops of my life.)

Five years ago, I was a blindly happy Calabasas house-wife who didn't know how to google, tweet, or text. #IgnoranceIsBliss. I was just like any normal mom who read celebrity tabloid magazines at the grocery store checkout merely for entertainment (and not to see if I was in any of them running my big mouth). Other than being the best mom and wife I could be and raising my children to become proper gentlemen one day, I had no real career or identity of my own. At that time, I had already achieved every goal I *thought* I wanted.

Guess what: Life goes on after reaching MILF status—one of the few labels I actually welcome. Today, I'm no longer that gullible housewife; I just play one on TV. (Thanks, Andy Cohen!)

Life has a funny way of working itself out.

I've been in the public eye now for a few years, and while I've definitely learned my fair share of lessons (like overly cross your legs yoga style when you get out of a car, never go outside without makeup, and *always* be nice to the paparazzi), there are some things I just won't get used to.

For instance, I'll never enjoy learning incredibly pri-vate things about my personal life from the cover of a magazine. #UsWeekly. Of course, I might end up running my mouth about it later, but call me crazy, I'd just like to be the first to know. Last year, I discovered, much to my surprise, that I was an unfaithful wife.

According to the report, I had sex with some guy in my family home six weeks after my second son was born. *Really? Six weeks?*

Now, as all of you ladies who have children know, doctors order *at least* that long before your kitty is even ready for sex (not to get all *National Geographic*, but I think it's more like twelve). And seriously, who feels hot enough or confident enough about her body to sleep with a new partner a month and a half after she's had a child? At that point, you're probably too embarrassed to even have sex with your own husband, let alone some hot stranger. Oh, not to mention that for the first two months I had a house filled with family, a round-the-clock baby nurse, and a full-time nanny, all the while dealing with postpartum depression. I mean, who comes up with this shit? Seriously, let's think about it. Who on earth would have *anything* to gain by leaking false information about an alleged affair *seven* days before the tell-all book about my philandering ex and his mistress hit bookstores? Hmm. You tell me.

To top that, my "affairs" were apparently with former NBA player Rick Fox, who I don't believe I've actually ever met, and restaurateur Harry Morton. Knowing what I do now about what a sham my marriage was, I may have welcomed dating either one of these eligible bachelors, but it just wasn't true.

Did I casually and frequently date before my divorce was finalized and my husband was already in a public relationship with another woman? Hell, yes, I did. Did I ever have an affair before that? No. Not ever. That's just not in my DNA. #ForBetterOrWorse.

I'll never get used to reading false claims about my personal life in the press, but I also appreciate the opportunities that being in the public eye has afforded me. It's what I signed up for and what ultimately helped save my life.

Only recently have I *truly* started putting myself out there again in the dating world with an open mind and, more importantly, an open heart. I needed time alone and time to find myself. I needed to figure out who the fuck I was. I had one serious relationship shortly after my divorce that opened my eyes and taught me how to have fun again because apparently life does exist outside The Valley after the age of thirty. However, I've mostly remained guarded and terrified of being hurt again. While opening my mind was a relatively easy task, you're about to find out I had a bit more trouble opening my heart.

At forty years old (going on twenty-five), I was finally ready to be a single woman again, but I had zero idea what to expect. To put it quite simply, the game has changed. You heard it here first, folks. If you're like me and have recently reentered the dating pool as a single parent or divorcée, you're in for a serious fucking wake-up call. Oh, you're married or in a long-term relationship and think this doesn't apply to you? Well, go fuck yourself. Knowing how to play the game—or that there even needs to be one—is just as important for keeping your partner as it is for landing him or her in the first place. #KeepItSexy. After thirteen years with the same man, I was finally off the bench and ready to play a few innings.

First, I had to figure out what I wanted in a partner. I've always had a type: tall, dark, and handsome. Since my relationship with my ex turned out to be an absolute disaster, I figured that it was a good idea to cast a wider net. I decided no type of guy was off-limits (except the taken ones!) and adopted the mantra "Yes is the new no!" It's been a liberating experience; it's also gotten me into a little bit of trouble (like, maybe *don't* say yes to skinny-dipping on a public beach after your third glass of wine). Because of my new outlook, I've gotten to know some really amazing men—and some pretty serious douche bags as well. My list of possible suitors ranged from twenty-three to fifty-six years old and was comprised of a film director, surfers, a felon, artists, D-list TV actors, real estate agents, a few not-so-closeted gay men, and—*gasp!*—even a couple of movie stars.

The next thing I needed to figure out was *how* to date in this technology-infused world. Of course, I knew that certain things would never change, like always keep your kitty cat fresh, never be too available, and just say no to booty calls. I mean, I was married to an actor for eight years; I wasn't dead. But learning to date again now is a whole new animal . . . and I'm not just talking "cougar."

When I first discovered the benefits of technology and social media, I used it to obsess about my husband, his future wife, and our children throughout our breakup and divorce. Once I decided I was open to love again, I realized that technology is also a very powerful—and dangerous—tool. Gone is the time of the "three-day rule." #SoLast Century. Today, it's rare to actually pick up the phone and call someone. Even my own voice mail instructs callers to text me instead—my in-box is always full.

Instead, we text, tweet, Facebook-message, and whatever other social fucking media I choose not to know about. #WhatTheFuckIsLinkedIn? I'm still trying to figure out Twitter. And that's just the tip of the iceberg (and at forty, who still plays "just the tip"?).

Barely surviving my divorce taught me that health, happiness, and *honesty* are the key ingredients to any successful union. It may sound obvious, but only after you learn to accept and forgive your own flaws and shortcomings can you forgive those in another individual. Face it, people, no one is perfect. Only after you let go of the pain in your past, can you have a future with someone new. Only after you've spent countless hours with some battery-operated bedroom toys can you fully direct your partner on what your exact needs are. And once you've conquered all of this, you're finally ready to share yourself, imperfections and all, with another person who will undoubtedly have just as many flaws of his or her own.

So join me in this new, unpredictable adventure, as I fumble through the dating world as a single parent, divorcée, reality personality, and just unlucky gal who occasionally gets lucky. Who hasn't experienced a nip slip or two? I mean, it's not like I started my reality career with a sex tape . . . but after all, I wouldn't be me without my fair share of mistakes. At the better judgment of my publisher, agent, and mother, some of the names and details of certain people have been changed to protect the privacy of the innocent . . . and not so innocent.

Here are a few of my favorite lessons learned:

1. Bathroom hookups are great ideas in theory— but a little less practical when there are cameras filming your every move. #RHOBH.

2. It doesn't matter how much money you have. Every woman gets wrinkly elbows eventually, and there's no such thing as knee lifts. Trust me, I've checked. #DoctorsKnowBest.

3. You should never kiss and tell, especially when it's a really famous Scottish actor and you're on live television. #KnowWhenToPleadTheFifth.

4. Finally, when you write an entire *cunt*-ry album about your affair with a married man, most people won't buy it. #JustSayin.

I Survived.
Now What?

THE VALLEY (NOUN)

1. A northern suburban area of Los Angeles where white picket fences and PebbleTec pools are synonymous with antidepressants, cheating spouses, and gossipy housewives.

2. The seventh ring of hell.

Example: After the former actress abandoned all hope for her once-thriving career, she resigned herself to living in The Valley.

I finally made it!

In Los Angeles, where you live is almost as important as who you know—or who you're fucking. And my new home is in the ultra-swanky Bel Air neighborhood (you'll learn more later about who I've been fucking).

After all these years, I was finally on the "right" side of Mulholland Drive—the iconic, windy road that sits on the top of the Santa Monica Mountains and separates L.A. proper from—*gasp!*—The Valley. It's the infamous road where old-time mobsters used to "dispose" of informants, where Charlie Sheen wrecked a car or four, and where I had a few close calls of my own. #NoDrivingAndTweeting.

You may be thinking I sound like a total brat, but I've paid my dues in LaLa Land. Don't be fooled by all the sunshine and pretty people: Hollywood can chew you up and spit you out faster than another new iPhone comes out. It's a city where people measure you by your appearance, your contacts, and your bank account as opposed to your character. So even if you don't got it, you *have* to flaunt it— especially when it comes to Hermès bags, zip codes, and fancy cars (which are generally leased). That shit is expensive! #FakeItTillYouMakeIt.

When it comes to domestic life, you can tell a lot by a person based solely on where he or she lives. The impossibly hip twenty-somethings and tormented unemployed actors live in the gritty Los Feliz and Silver Lake areas. The gays, celebrity wannabes, and star-fucking cocktail waitresses rent overpriced studio apartments in the heart of West Hollywood. The not-so-struggling artists reside in the canals of Venice Beach. The incredibly rich and famous stake their claim in Beverly Hills, Bel Air, and Malibu. This is how L.A. slices and dices.

When I first moved to Los Angeles with my friend Michelle in 1995, we rented a studio apartment on Doheny Drive and Sunset Boulevard in West Hollywood (yes, we fell into *that* category) with a single full-size bed, a hot plate, and a nearby pay phone we used as a landline. The scene was so unlike what we were used to in Europe, where we used to model, or even San Francisco. All the women seemed to look the same: blond hair, big lips, and even bigger boobs. In the modeling world, your unique traits are celebrated. Los Angeles seemed like a virtual silicone assembly line churning out one Pamela Anderson–inspired look-alike after another. After about a year of "roughing it" in our tiny apartment, our very rich, very Persian male friend—who we used to do some major partying with in San Francisco—offered to contribute half of our rent for a nicer apartment provided that whenever he visited L.A. we would be his token arm candy and help him get into all the cool clubs and events. (He would have never gotten in without being flanked by a couple of models.) #ShahOfSanFran. At twenty-three years old, it sounded like a fantastic idea and not the least bit like a platonic escort service. Let the record show, neither Michelle nor I ever slept with him—in fact, he's still a close friend of mine today. Like lots of guys, he just wanted to be around a couple of pretty young models and, like most girls, we just wanted our own bedrooms, telephones inside our apartment, and a fancy meal once in a while. #WinWin.

Soon after I met the charming "made for TV" actor who would one day become my philandering ex-husband, he whisked me away from my place on the Westside to his Toluca Lake condo—my first taste of Valley life. Anyone raised in the eighties knows the movie *Valley Girl*—it's where the brooding hunk from Hollywood falls for the bubbly popular girl from the wrong side of the hill. There was a certain social stigma attached to the valleys of L.A. Today, it's actually hip to live in certain areas of The Valley, but it still produces a wrinkled nose from most 90210-ers. When I told my friends I was moving to Toluca Lake, they felt the need to say something consoling like "I'm sure it won't be forever," "At least you'll be close to the Hollywood Bowl," or "You can get some fabulous shoes with all the money you're saving." I mean, I wasn't moving to fucking Siberia.

But at the time I would have taken a bullet for that man, so I didn't care. Let me rephrase, I didn't care enough *not* to move. In the years that followed, we started moving further and further east down the Hollywood Freeway. We eventually landed in Encino for five years, but the final kiss of death was when he packed up our perfect little family and moved us to the deepest part of The Valley: Cala-fucking-basas. For those of you who have never heard of the town, it's a ritzy and exclusive enclave for those north of Mulholland. #KrisJenner. There was one grocery store, a single movie theater, and two restaurants—all of which were closed by nine P.M. Our real estate agent told us the town was dubbed "the land of horses and divorces," because everything for sale in the area was either bare land or the product of yet another failed marriage. Honestly, it's pretty easy to blame your partner for everything when there's nothing fucking else to do.

While it wasn't my dream come true, we did have a massive house in a gated community with a huge backyard complete with a giant waterslide, a sports court, and a half-acre fruit orchard—amenities that would have cost us at least triple in the 90210. Our home was roughly twenty-five miles from West Hollywood, but with L.A. traffic it was *at least* an hour drive at any given time of day, so I was trapped in Housewives Hell. Not that it wasn't pretty and pristine, but there were more bored housewives per square mile there than in a pole-dancing strip class. #GuiltyAs Charged. Every husband was fucking somebody else's wife, and antidepressants might as well have been popped with a PEZ dispenser. I referred to the gates that enclosed our beautiful community as my own personal *Truman Show* (including the fake husband) or, if you prefer, *Groundhog*

Day. Either way, I quickly became my own version of a Stepford wife.

My ex-husband frequented the other side of the hill several times a week for auditions, golf, "meetings," and poker (translation: poke her) games. He rarely invited me to go with him. And it's clear now that he just didn't want to risk me running into any of his girlfriends or former one-night stands—but you got enough of that in the first book, and the idea of rehashing it all only makes me want to fucking scream.

After my divorce, the boys and I bounced around from rental to rental in Encino because it was close enough to my friends on the Westside and I could still get to Calabasas in a decent amount of time. For the sake of my kids I decided to keep the boys at the same school they had been attending prior to our divorce, but it was just too unhealthy for me to stay there, because every bored housewife knew my pathetic cheating husband story. I was the talk of every nail salon and Pilates class for nearly two years—and now, thanks to *Real Housewives of Beverly Hills,* a frequent subject even today. But my kids have always and will always come first. They had already dealt with enough change, so keeping them with their friends was important to me. Living in Encino was my own personal compromise.

After two years in my second Encino rental, a quarter mile north of Mulholland (#StillTheValley), I had finally saved up enough money to find a nicer place where we could each have our own room—and I could get the fuck out of the 818 area code. My life had finally come full circle.

My real estate agent and I pulled into the driveway of this seventies-esque four-bedroom home, and I could feel my heartbeat quicken. It was elegant, spacious, and, most importantly, one block *south* of Mulholland. #BelAir. It meant my friends couldn't use "The Valley is just so far" as an excuse not to visit anymore.

We walked through the large, wooden double doors into a marble foyer with high ceilings, and it immediately felt like home. The walls were painted a soft shade of yellow that made me smile. I wandered from room to room before locking eyes on two French doors that opened to a yard with a bright blue sparkling swimming pool. My youngest son is a fish (#WatchOutPhelps), and I knew he would be over the moon that his mom's house would have a pool just like his dad's house. (I'm still working on getting them that movie theater.) For me, the real selling point was the master bedroom. It had not one, but *two* walk-in closets, plus a third bonus closet. Most women would chew off their right arm for three closets. It doesn't even matter if you have enough shit to fill them. I thought I had stepped into heaven. When I walked into the master bath, I gasped. It had my holy grail . . . a steam shower! *Holy fuck*, I thought, *I made it!* I had steam showers at both of the homes I shared with Eddie and became quickly addicted to them. My earlier rentals over the years barely had enough hot water for a ten-minute shower, let alone any kind of steam. In an odd way I felt like my life had finally moved forward, all because of this silly bathroom! Not to mention, the bedroom area was large enough for my stripper pole, which my kids think is a super-cool fireman pole. (It was an anniversary gift from my ex-husband that I'm all too happy to use without him.) I *had* to have this house.

My Bel Air dream home was spitting distance from my previous rental, but it felt like it was a thousand miles away. Maybe I'm imagining it, but the sun shines a little brighter and birds sing a little sweeter on the south side of Mulholland. I know this all sounds insanely superficial, and it is, but it was a huge personal victory for me that I never thought I would have again. All the hard work of these last five painful years was finally paying off. It symbolized my independence. My ex-husband banished me to a faraway land deep in The Valley to lock me up like Rapunzel, but now I was free to decide where the fuck *I* wanted to live and what the fuck *I* wanted to do with my life. In some ways, it was like cutting his final leash of ownership over me. It wasn't a mansion by any stretch of the imagination—but I fucking loved it.

My best friend Jennifer Giminez came to help me unpack the day we moved in. When I saw her walking up the driveway, I ran outside to greet her and screamed, "This is it! I got it back!" We started jumping up and down and dancing around like twelve-year-old girls. I felt whole again. After years of stumbling, crawling, and barely getting by (including one nasty stiletto injury), I was finally pulling my shit together—and this house was proof that I had weathered a very rocky storm.

Rebuilding my life wasn't easy. While I was going through the darkest days of our divorce, many of my friends were getting married and starting families. "I'll have another glass" became my signature phrase at weddings and baby showers. When I was no longer included in "couples dinners," which still happens by the way (because God forbid I arrive without a partner), I'd spend lonely nights where I'd relapse so bad into my skin-picking addiction that I'd wake up the next morning with my face looking like a pepperoni pizza.

But with the help of *real* friends, a whole lot of white and rosé wine, some antidepressants, and the occasional chemical peel, I've been able to shed my old skin and begin again. I've said it before: I don't completely believe that we're meant to be with the same partner for the rest of our lives. I know that sounds cynical, and it's not to say it can't be done, but at this point in my life marriage just isn't for me. (I'd like to retain the option to change my mind. #HalleBerry.) From what I've seen, ten years is about as long as it lasts. In Los Angeles, being committed for ten years should earn you a purple fucking heart in addition to half of everything. It turns out that being married for eight years doesn't entitle you to that much, so stick it out. #HindsightIs20-20. Regardless of who you are or where you live, once the honeymoon is over, long-term relationships are usually an uphill battle (but hey, at least you'll have great leg and ass definition!).

Seriously, though, show me the "perfect relationship" and I'll show you a relationship you don't know anything about. You have to do what works for you, whether it's threesomes, dress-up, or something else. Don't be judge-y assholes, people!

Sure, I had achieved major milestones as a single, independent woman, but when it comes to men, I'm still extremely insecure, and being vulnerable again scares the shit out of me. The idea of tying myself to one person after finally freeing myself of my ex-husband's restraint makes me want to vomit. Why would I run the risk of going all the way back to square one? I attempted to use each milestone—like a fancy new house—as proof that I didn't need a partner.

Here's why:

It's pretty much common knowledge that women tend

to be more capable of monogamous relationships than men. Why else would some guy's "commitment issues" be a plot point for countless TV shows and movies? Women are preconditioned to believe that a man's greatest fear is being trapped into commitment and that a woman's mission is to trap him. (Ladies, never tell a man that your "clock is ticking." #NotHot.) Given my relationship history, I wasn't sure I could jump on that roller-coaster ride again.

Welcome to the Birdcage Theory.

People often joke that marriage is like being in a prison, but I disagree (even though many of my friends refer to their husbands as the Warden). There aren't any windows in a prison cell, and for the most part, you're living in your own personal hell. I prefer to think of marriage as being in a birdcage—with a locked door. You have a 360-degree view of everything going on in the world around you, but when you're married, you're no longer able to participate in it as you did before. When you're in a relationship, but opt not to marry, the door is always open and you know the option is there but generally choose not to leave. Once that cage door shuts and locks, you become restless. Soon, you feel the bars closing in around you—even if your particular cage has a fancy birdbath, a four-car garage, and a beautiful canary to share it with. You panic and decide that God gave you wings for a fucking reason, so it's time to break the fuck out.

Fuck the clank of the cage door slamming shut! Never again did I want to be anyone's captured little birdie. I have wings and I want to use them. I convinced myself that I didn't need a fucking man to tie me down. But one looming question remained: Now that I survived, where would my wings take me?

Figuring that out has been terrifying, but incredibly gratifying. I was lucky. When I needed it most, the chance of a lifetime came along that would change me (or at least my bank account) for the better—an opportunity I would never have had if it hadn't been for my messy public divorce, which was splashed across the pages of magazines for the world to see. I figured, why would I need to date anyone when I could have a reality-TV marriage to Bravo?

In 2012, I became a full-fledged Housewife on Bravo's hit series *The Real Housewives of Beverly Hills*. Being cast on one of television's most popular reality shows was an opportunity to show people that I wasn't some crazy-ass bitch (okay, maybe a *little* bit of a crazy bitch). Hobbling into that cougar den—on one stiletto and crutches—was a walk in the park compared to what I had already gone through in my real life. Seriously, I'd already lived a tabloid scandal, so a few bitchy Housewives couldn't scare me away. Until this show came along, I was labeled nothing more than a scorned ex-wife. Let's face it, we're a dime a dozen and that label is *not* hot. This television series gave me the chance to show people who I really am—the good, the bad, and the occasionally ugly. For better or worse, I'm basically who you see on TV. I'm the first one to tell you that I'm not perfect, and even though you're reading this book, I'm probably not the best person to be doling out relationship advice. Everybody knows I run my mouth way too much and sometimes I'm right—but not always. #SorryKimRichards. I hope that's why people who watch the show can relate to me. I believe on some level that everybody is a little fucked up. Finally, I had a chance to put an end to the "divorce scandal" that once defined me.

Instead, I went from one new controversy to the next— one after the other. People were really paying me to open my big, fat mouth? Seriously? We all know about the "meth" accusation heard around the reality world and the absolute "horror" when my youngest son, Jake, dropped his pants to pee on the lawn at a pool party. (Side note: Jake's bathroom habits haven't evolved that much. He stills sneaks in a grass watering whenever he can. #BoysWill BeBoys.) When I returned to *RHOBH* in season three, there was no shortage of drama. First, I was labeled as a "whore" because I made out with a hot guy in the bathroom at a party at one A.M. Go ahead and sue me! I freely admit that this totally happened. Were we having sex? Absolutely not. My fellow Housewife Lisa Vanderpump stopped us before we even had the chance! That's not to say we wouldn't have—it was late and we were drinking—but it was as innocent as it could have been. I didn't realize that two grown-ass adults kissing in a private room would be such an issue for these women. I guess I should have known better with a group of ladies who feign repulsion when little boys pee in a bush or when they hear the word *fuck*. Come on, we'll all say it! (Side note: That guy I made out with in the bathroom? We ended up dating.)

Last year, I was accused of breaking up a "made for TV" marriage. That's something I don't take too lightly. While I don't 100 percent believe in marriage for myself at this point, I still have the utmost respect for what it means and the extreme commitment it involves. My parents have been married for more than forty-five years, and I hope that if my boys choose to marry one day (but not for a really, really, really long time), it will be just as successful. By my own admission, I shared something private about my former cast mate that I shouldn't have with a group of women—most of whom already knew—that eventually trickled into the press, but I won't repeat it again. I was wrong. I know all too well the pit I get in my stomach when I hear that people have been gossiping about my family. In my defense, it was the worst-kept secret in Beverly Hills. If it wasn't, how the hell would I have known about it? After all, I was from The Valley.

The demise of this marriage was a sad fucking story

line for three seasons of *Real Housewives*, so how was it my fucking fault? If one person's words have the power to completely destroy a relationship, wasn't it doomed anyway? From where I stand, it looks like both parties have moved way the fuck on. (Maybe they need a little guidance on being newly single in LaLa Land. Perhaps I'll send them a copy of this book. #WhyNot?)

Divorce is as common in Beverly Hills as BOTOX, Black Cards, and Bentleys. (Have I mentioned that everyone in this town loves to fuck everyone else? Just as long as it's not the person they're married to.) So it wasn't really a surprise that my experience became a large part of the conversation among my newest TV friends. It turned out that one of the many women who had slept with my husband was an employee at Villa Blanca—a restaurant owned by one of my cast mates. I had no intention of ever speaking with this person. Besides sharing the same dick for a few years, we had absolutely nothing in common and nothing to talk about. Even calling *any* kind of attention to her in this book makes me cringe, but it's something people ask me about a lot. How was I able to sit down with this person? How could I look her in the eye? She knew he was married. She knew he had children. But she kept fucking him anyway. Three reasons. First, I had already done it with my ex's new wife. My close friend had asked me to so that it could help her with her new spin-off reality show, and I'm actually a very reasonable person and a generous friend. Second, while I don't feel sorry for that silly fucking cocktail waitress, I know my ex-husband fucked her over too. She went through her own heartbreak (which she deserved), and for the rest of her life when someone googles her name, she'll be identified as the girl who sleeps with married men—and John Mayer—and who sold all the tawdry details to the press. We'll never be friends, but I had moved on, so if some random cocktail waitress needed closure from *me* because she fucked *my* ex-husband, I would give her that. And third, of all the women who fucked my husband while we were together (and there were many), she was the only one to apologize. That doesn't make seeing the bitch at every Lisa Vanderpump event any less shitty. Apparently, she's getting married now (although that didn't stop her from flirting with my date all night long at a recent dinner party—on camera). I only hope she never has to experience firsthand what I endured.

All the drama aside, this show helped me build a new life, and I wouldn't be where I am today without it. I also credit it for helping me *eventually* see that I want and deserve a partner of my own (see chapter 2), partly because of all those parties where I had someone's husband screaming in my face. I have zero problem standing up for myself, but I would have welcomed having a teammate in those particular instances.

As a result of most of the shit I've been through, I have discovered that I can handle just about anything—because, like the saying goes, "time heals all wounds."

But time can also be a really nasty bitch.

Everyone knows that *fuck* is one of my favorite words: Fuck me, fuck you, fuck off, and fuck it. It really does make every sentence or phrase sound better. #TrustMe. Some people think it's crass or vulgar, but I know a much dirtier "F" word: *forty*. I mean, motherfucking forty!

Getting older is inevitable, but I still think aging can suck a fat dick. People who say, "Forty is the new thirty," can suck it. Just look at our knees. Forty-year-old knees are not the new thirty. I never had armpits that looked like vaginal labia when I was thirty. I never needed to get fillers in my hands when I was thirty. And if I'm being truly honest with myself, maybe some of my reluctance to date again was because of my age. In this superficial city, hot young guys want to fuck cougars—they don't want to commit to them. Even sixty-year-old men want the hot thirty-somethings or even the twenty-somethings. Had I already reached my expiration date? Would I be resigned to picking up my future partner at a bunco tournament before heading to his granddaughter's bat mitzvah? I *seriously* don't want to be a "bonus" grandma just yet. I'm sure you think I'm being totally irrational, but when have I ever let common sense get in the way?

By the time this book is released, I'll have had another birthday . . . but for the sake of my own sanity, let's keep the age talk to a minimum. (Kidding. I will obsess over it through this entire book.) But I do believe if you feel young and cute, you are young and cute. Case fucking closed.

Being a former model means that I'm probably more critical of body changes than most people. I spent so much of my life being overscrutinized, analyzed under a microscope, picked apart, and criticized by some of the most ruthless agents, managers, and designers in the modeling business. "You're not a face girl" was a common phrase I heard at casting auditions. #FuckYou. I used to be so hard on myself (and certain bloggers and gossip websites can be incredibly cruel), but now I try to accept where I am in my life and appreciate the silver linings when I can find them.

Here are some reasons I try to be happy about the real "F" word:

1. Sex is way better. As a grown woman, I know exactly what I want, and being satisfied has never "cum" so easy.

2. Cameron Diaz, Christy Turlington, Heidi Klum, Kate Moss, Halle Berry, and Salma Hayek. All of these women are in their forties, and all of them are incredibly sexy. #GoodCompany.

3. I no longer feel obligated to deal with other people's garbage or feel shame about popping a Lexapro when needed. I've adopted the motto "Do what you gotta do to make it through."

4. If I'm in need of a little cosmetic enhancement, I can afford to fix it myself. And a little timely maintenance (#Fillers, #Botox, #Boobs) can go a long way in avoiding ever having to have a face-lift.

5. If I work out hard enough and think positive, confident thoughts—my head and my ass can still be twenty-five. #YoungAtHeart.

At long last, all the loose ends in my life were finally tying together into a perfectly imperfect pink bow. I was finally at peace with my divorce and happy with my career, my zip code, my body, and almost my age. I couldn't possibly ask for anything more . . . could I?

Brandi's

ENJOY LIFE NOW BECAUSE THE SPECIAL OCCASION YOU'RE SAVING THAT BOTTLE OF DOM FOR MAY TAKE SO LONG, WHEN IT'S FINALLY OPENED, IT'S SOURED. #HAPPENEDTOME.

Tweet-ism

2

Table for One

SCORNED (ADJ.)

A label placed on a woman who has suffered a particularly nasty breakup or divorce, and therefore, must be a bitter, broken bitch.

Example: When her husband ran off with his twenty-something assistant, the now-single mother of three was referred to as a "scorned ex-wife" for relying on antidepressants and vocalizing her distrust in men.

I want to scream every time I hear someone refer to me as a "scorned ex-wife." It implies that I'm damaged goods or something—or worse, that it was somehow irrational for me to be absolutely furious that my marriage went up in a ball of fucking flames. He screwed half of Hollywood and *I'm* the one with this bullshit motherfucking label? I'm the crazy bitch because he couldn't keep his dick in his pants to save his life—or, at the very least, his marriage?

Looking back now, maybe for the first few years after our divorce I was scorned because after my world dissolved and my family was torn apart, I wanted to blame my ex-husband for every pill I ever popped. He was the reason I could single-handedly keep a BevMo! in business. I convinced myself that the heartache he caused me was the reason I sat in a Beverly Hills jail cell overnight after getting slapped with a charge of driving under the influence. At the time, I rationalized that it was because of his bad decisions that my landlord was hiking up our rent and the boys and I were forced to move yet again, but this time with only two weeks' notice. Everything was his fault. I truly believed in my battered and beaten heart that it was because of him that I was a fucking mess. It was because of every lie he ever told me and every whore he ever fucked that I had zero credit, zero education, and zero identity. It was entirely his fault. . . .

Or was it? I made the decision to go blindly into the fairy tale without anything to fall back on and no assurance of a life if, God forbid, our marriage didn't work out. Could I really blame him because I made the decision to quit modeling and follow him around the world? Could I blame him that I wasn't able to repay my parents for everything they did for me? Was he the reason that I tripped over my own stiletto and shattered the bones in my ankle and leg?

Of course it wasn't *really* his fault. I knew better, but in those dark, depressing moments it was easier to blame him than to let him go completely. Being angry with my ex-husband was just another excuse I used to keep fucking up. I could forgive all of my cringe-worthy missteps, because in some way I *deserved* to be a basket case. It was my rite of passage. It was like I was living tribute to Alanis Morissette's angry chick rock: "I'm *here* to remind you / of the mess you left when you went away!"

Having a person to hate and blame filled some void inside me when I felt so empty. My husband was gone, but I didn't yet have anyone to replace him with, so I sank into the ground and wallowed. Clinging to stale anger created a place for him in my postmarried (some call it divorced) life. In some twisted way, having him be the object of my rage kept me connected to him. Meanwhile, my ex-husband transitioned, relatively smoothly, to a new, seemingly happy life. He jumped immediately into a serious, *seemingly* committed relationship with his mistress and went on his married fucking way. And I was alone.

It took me 1,825 days to figure out that *I* was the reason I hadn't moved on. *I* was the reason I hadn't opened my life to someone new. I had done more damage to my-self by simply reacting to his actions rather than moving on from them. But at the end of the day, I was still dam-aged. I had suffered the ultimate betrayal, and I navigated myself through it. The cold hard truth: I had become my own worst enemy.

Let's get serious. The only person I could hold *really* accountable for drinking so much that I stumbled out of a restaurant with the top of my pretty Alice + Olivia dress pulled down showing my boob and the bottom tucked up to reveal a black thong with my tampon string hanging out, was most definitely all me. Truthfully, I don't regret that much of it—especially those mile-high, super-hot Lanvin heels that put me on crutches for over three months. I truly feel my broken leg was God's way of tell-ing me to slow the fuck down and get my shit together. My ex-husband should have stopped being my problem the moment I accepted that our marriage was over. After that, it was all on Brandi. Today, I only blame him for the things that are actually his fault, like losing our kids' pass-ports, giving the boys really terrible haircuts, lashing out at *me* when Mason comes home with a bad grade, forget-ting to put money in Jakey's hot lunch account at school; causing the boys' growing cavity count, and generally blaming me for his own "insert pathetic country song title here" misery.

On the outside—and to those friends and family around me—it looked like I had finally gotten my shit together. Despite the occasional nip slip, I had dusted myself off quite nicely. But I'll let you in on a little secret: I fucking hate being alone. I think putting on a front was a way to help me get through the days and nights when I was *so* depressed and pathetically sad. I am, in fact, a hopeless romantic. I want someone to wake up with each morning, to take out the trash on garbage day, and to care deeply about me. I wanted my date on New Year's Eve to be the same man who took me out on Valentine's Day.

The fact of the matter is that I actually wholeheartedly really love men. I just no longer trust any of them—not in any way, shape, or form. After all that happened in my marriage, how could I stop my mind from going down a dark, suspicious path whenever my boyfriend wanted a guys' night out? I mean, the saying "Trust your gut" came from somewhere, right? Moving forward, will I actually consider going through a guy's phone and reading his text messages? Nope, that's just not me. I'm sure I'm better than that—at least I hope I am. But why is this idea even crossing my mind? After the first suspicion, should I just cut the cord and break it off before I have the chance to get hurt again? If I'm not officially with a man, he can't actually cheat on me—because we haven't placed a label on our relationship or discussed exclusivity. Welcome to my fucked-up mind, people.

Let me give you an example of my crazy: I was dating this guy for a few months, and we were really hitting it off. He said and did all the right things (well, most of the time), but given my new "reality" living in the public eye, I couldn't help but question his motives. One day, I casually asked him if he ever had any dreams of pursuing acting or being in the entertainment business. I noticed he had a professional head shot as his Facebook profile— anyone living in Los Angeles who has a professional picture of himself, whether it's on social media or at home in a photo album, has at one time at least thought about pursuing some kind of career in the spotlight.

He swore to me that he had zero interest in anything Hollywood related—but was all too eager when I asked him if he'd be interested in filming with me for the show, even though he wouldn't be compensated and nothing was really in it for him besides being on television. (Side note: This has become a common occurrence in my life. More gay men than I care to count have asked me out because they're hoping dating me would allow them access to all things *Housewives* . . . and Bravo. Maybe they were really after Andy?) Needless to say, I was mistrusting of his motives in our relationship so I did what any rational, suspicious gal would do: I found myself some insurance in

case he did turn out to be a fame whore. #ParanoiaSelf
Destroya.

If you're newly dating someone, the best way to find
out more about this person is to raid his motherfucking
medicine cabinet (trust me on this). It's where people keep
all their secrets, so you'll learn more about him in thirty
seconds than you probably could in thirty dates. May I
suggest staying in bed one morning after he has left for
work. The line "You wore me out so good, I need more
sleep" works every time. Once you're alone, do a little bit
of snooping. I'm not talking about hacking into a person's
e-mail, researching his Internet history, or anything
crazy; I'm talking about the shit that actually might have
an effect on you since you're sleeping with that person
(case in point: the medicine cabinet). If he is taking medi-
cation for a particular disease, virus, or disorder, you damn
sure have the right to know about it!

That's exactly what I did. I grabbed my phone, snapped
pictures of every prescription bottle, making sure to get
the part of the label with his name and address on it, and
sent them to my e-mail. I'm familiar with the name of
most medications, but some of these generic names were
throwing me for a loop. I sent the photos to myself so that
I could google them later when I got home. Listen, if this
guy was putting *his* business all up in *my* business, then I
had every right to know what kind of meds he was on.

Plus, it was some ass-backward form of protection in case he ever tried to fuck me over. Blackmail *is* totally normal, right? #RealityTVTaughtMeWell.

Just because I don't want to get married again doesn't mean I don't want a life partner. What I've realized is really quite simple: I have to learn to trust again—no matter how impossible that may seem—because if I don't, I may never find true happiness in love again. Having my heart crushed was beyond devastating. My divorce didn't just rock my life; it shook everybody who was a part of it—my parents, siblings, in-laws, friends, and, most tragically, my children. I wasn't sure if I could ever survive that again—I barely got out of that one alive—so I was terrified to take that risk again. But I was going to have to try.

So, after one particular breakup, I remember asking myself what went wrong. This guy and I only dated a few short weeks, and he had so much going for him. He was intelligent, attractive, financially and emotionally stable, and so on, but I pushed him away before things could get too serious. It was my self-protection kicking in. We had good chemistry and it probably could have developed into something deeper, but when I learned that his job required him to spend a few weeks a quarter on the East Coast, I called it off. I immediately began imagining how I would feel during those weeks he was gone. What if he decided to start dating a girl in New York too? (Or worse, what if he already had a girl there and I was just his West Coast girlfriend?) How would I react if I found that out? The what-ifs started building that cage around me, and I started to panic.

My paranoia was getting the best of me and I began spiraling into crazy girlfriend mode, and that's never hot to a man. So I did what any fucking coward would do. I called him a few days before he left and let him down softly, sweetly, and, most importantly, first. He couldn't crush my heart if I was the one to break things off. I told him that it would be for the best if we didn't see each other anymore. We were supposed to meet for dinner that night and he was wondering if we could talk about it in person.

"I don't think so," I said, almost doubting the words the moment they crossed my lips, but I knew I had to be resolute in my decision.

He was confused but accepted it. What else could he do? Part of me was satisfied that I hurt him before he could hurt me. But part of me was hurting anyway, because I didn't want to break up with him. I just didn't think I had any other choice.

I spent that evening at home alone with a glass of Whispering Angel and turned to Google for support. That's what people do nowadays, right? There were countless websites and blog posts dedicated to "How Can I Trust Again?" Most of it was psychobabble nonsense—the kind of shit your mom told you after a high school heartbreak that sounded right but never actually worked. The search mostly produced numbered lists that included things like "Spend time nurturing yourself," "You're only the victim if you allow yourself to be," and "Your past is not your future." Blah blah blah. It was all garbage. #Trash. My past was affecting every little aspect of my future. It turns out the Internet can be your worst enemy— especially when you spend most of your time googling medical conditions, surviving cheating, or reviewing the Twitter feed of some *cunt*-ry music singer who likes to post countless pictures of your children. #Stillbugs.

At the end, the answer was simple: there was no answer. Ultimately, if I truly wanted to trust someone again, I would just have to try and hope the person I wanted to take that giant leap for was worth the risk and worthy of my heart.

Once I had that epiphany, so to speak, I realized that I needed to hop back on the dating horse or bicycle, whichever is safer. Before I could ever consider trusting someone else with my heart, I had to get a better idea of what I wanted in a partner at this stage in my life. When I was twenty-three years old, my ex-husband was my dream man, and having someone give me butterflies was my only criteria other than tall, dark, and handsome. Okay, to be honest, he was basically everyone's dream man. I lived in blissful ignorance for thirteen wonderful years (not realizing he was having more affairs than Tiger Woods with only a fraction of the net worth), and then it went up in a ball of flames. I learned that for every middle-aged wife with nothing on her face but a scowl (a little mascara can go a long way, ladies), there's some random twenty-two-year-old cocktail waitress grinning ear to ear through her cheap red lipstick who is all too happy to stroke your husband's ego all day long. She's also most likely willing to stroke something else all night long. Listen, I know that not every devastatingly handsome man turns out to be a total douche bag—and even the ugly ones can be chronic cheaters.

I started by making a list of what my ideal partner should be:

1. Roughly five to eight years older than me, so I could avoid an Ashton/Demi-esque saga if it didn't end up working out.

2. Either divorced or formerly in at least one long-term, committed relationship (five years or more). Forty- and fifty-year-old men who have never been in a serious relationship scare the hell out of me. They should scare the hell out of you too. Those guys are completely desensitized and are perpetually searching for a "unicorn" but never want to settle (see chapter 11).

3. Successful in his career. I had already experienced enough men trying to use my position in the public eye to bolster their own image, so I want someone who is already established.

4. A parent, an animal lover, or, at the very least, a responsible plant owner. This one is important because it shows a man's ability and willingness to give to someone other than himself. Plus my boys and my puppies are the center of my world—even my demon dog, Buddy.

5. Someone who gives me butterflies. We should never settle for good enough, just because it's easier and more comfortable than being alone. I *deserve* to be swept off my feet. I want someone who inspires me to be a better version of myself. Who knows if that guy is really out there, but I'm going to keep on looking for my perfect man.

So now that I knew what kind of man I wanted, I needed to figure out how to fucking find him—or, more importantly, if he even existed. When it comes to dating, I realized that I am, shockingly, a traditionalist. Online dating has never been something that's interested me—and let's not ignore the giant elephant in the room: once you become a public personality, it's sort of hard to weed out the good guys from the fame-hungry manwhores. You can also forget about Tinder (which is a smart phone "hookup" app; the hetero equivalent of Grinder). So what the fuck am I supposed to do? Date some perfect stranger who I met at the gym and who spent an hour flexing his biceps in a floor-to-ceiling mirror? I think not.

The last time I was a single girl out on this town, it was 1995. I was twenty-three years old, and the idea of settling down was light-years away (or so I thought). Back then, finding a date for Saturday night was never difficult: my girlfriend and I would throw on the tiniest outfits we could find and strut over to our nightly haunt, the Sunset Marquis. We'd plant ourselves inside the tiny bar, cozy up to the bartender, and wait to see who would arrive that evening. We were a part of West Hollywood's "model posse," so naturally the boys gravitated our way. Most of the patrons were studio bigwigs or rock stars who always had a running bar tab, so we never bought our own drinks. #ThoseWereTheDays. *These* days, I am no longer just searching for some hot Hollywood hookup, so that's no longer my scene. (Trust me, I've had my fair share. Read about them in chapter 4.)

I asked myself (and many of my single girlfriends), where does a woman like me go to meet a good man? My first instinct was the golf course, naturally. The L.A. country clubs are riddled with reasonably fit, wealthy men with more than ample time to squeeze in eighteen holes before dinner. #TWSS. One tiny little problem: I don't golf. That's not to say I couldn't *learn* to golf. If going to the same restaurants and bars you frequently haunt isn't working for you, you need to go outside your comfort zone. But was I really ready to golf? I mean, I could definitely get behind tennis (the outfits are super-cute), but I'm not sure a polo shirt and knee-length khaki shorts would do much to enhance my figure.

Home Depot, I've decided, is one of the absolute best places to meet men. Manly men go to Home Depot—the kind who are hoping to *make* a woman a housewife, not the kind looking to date a "made for TV" one; the kind who like to open doors for ladies and build things with their rough, strong hands. Since there aren't a lot of single women roaming the electrical aisle, we can have our pick of the litter when it comes to Home Depot's most eligible bachelors. But be warned: a lot of bored husbands seek solace at Home Depot from overly nagging wives, so fully inspect every left hand for rings or tan lines. It's also one of the few places on earth where I allow myself to be a damsel in distress. Quite often I need help from a tall, handsome male shopper to pull something down from an impossibly high shelf. (This should go without saying, but *always* choose the item just out of your reach.) Growing up, I was a really girly girl and preferred to play with Barbies than building blocks, so I'm not that familiar with the tools you find in Home Depot. However, I am pretty familiar with the kind you find in nightclubs in West Hollywood. Needless to say, I can play the part of a damsel in distress and be desperately in need of help from the hunky guy nearby to find the perfect screwdriver. After which, we may go out for a proper screwdriver (the kind made with vodka). And when the sales associate asks if I need help carrying things to my car, the answer is always "yes!"

When you're tired of prowling the same five places you've had on steady rotation for six months, throw on your tightest pair of light-wash jeans and a white tank top (with perhaps a lacy, peekaboo black bra strap dangling out) and make a Saturday afternoon trip to Home Depot. If you stand around long enough looking lost, you're destined to meet a real man. #TrustMe.

Recently, I decided it was time to call in some reinforcement. I made an appointment with a Los Angeles–area matchmaker—a legitimate, old-school love guru—to set me up with my ideal mate, or at least a good date. She took into consideration a laundry list of things (including my requirements) along with my height, location, finances, interests, and family history, before embarking on her search. She explained that both parties would remain anonymous prior to meeting—which meant we wouldn't be able to google each other. #Yikes.

A week after my consultation, the matchmaker called to inform me that she had found a fantastic candidate for me to meet for dinner. This is when the first-date jitters started to kick in. I had never been on a blind date where I haven't been able to at least stalk Facebook beforehand. Two hours before we were supposed to meet, I was sitting in front of my bathroom mirror applying black eyeliner and I froze.

Holy shit, I thought. *This guy is so desperate to be in a relationship that he went to a fucking matchmaker!* #Hypocrite.

If the date went well and we started to see each other, would it be because he really liked me or because he was just so lonely and ready to settle for anyone who met his criteria? Just then, Jake waddled into the room and complained that he wasn't feeling well (it's a frequent trick he uses to get my attention when I'm putting on my makeup because he knows this means I'm getting ready to leave for the evening). I put my hand on his forehead . . . well, he did feel a *little* warm. I decided not to test it with a thermometer because we moms always know best and I was a little worried I might see the dreaded 98.6. Okay, so I totally chickened out and left a message for my matchmaker that my son had come down with a fever and I'd have to reschedule. I never called her again.

Looking back, I do regret not going on that date. He could have been the next great love of my life. He also could have been just another total douche bag. I realized I was going to have to go about this whole thing the old-fashioned way: throw on a sexy outfit and some strappy heels and force myself to be out on the town.

At the end of the day, I guess I do have one final thing I can blame my ex-husband for: having to learn how to fucking date again, as a single mom and a divorcée.

Brandi's

SCORNED IS THE NEW SCORCHING.
#REDHOTANDSINGLE.

Tweet-ism

3

Douche Bags,

Part One

DOUCHE BAG (NOUN)

1. An offensive man that lies, cheats, or is an all-around shady person.

2. Roughly 90 percent of the male population in Los Angeles.

Example: The guy you're dating is a total douche bag when he tells you you're the oldest girl he's ever dated.

Douche bags are everywhere. It's not an epidemic unique to Hollywood. However, the *type* of douche bags you encounter is relative to where you live. It's like baseball: every major city has a team, but the uniforms, the park, and the general style of game play depend on the town. The same goes for douche-y guys. For example, New York City has the pretentious Wall Street bankers rocking crocodile loafers with no socks and some of the Queens-bred slimeballs who still think yellow-gold pinky rings are fashionable accessories. Dallas has some of those "down-to-earth" cowboys who drive $70,000 pickup trucks and think a woman's place is to be seen and not heard. Miami and Las Vegas . . . do I even need to say it?

Then there's Hollywood. I like to think of Tinseltown as the douche bag capital of the world. It's a melting pot for some of the biggest assholes known to man. When I finally made the decision to start *seriously* opening myself up to having someone to share my life with, I realized that douches, like many things, only get worse with age. And when you're a single woman in L.A.—especially one known for making questionable decisions in the public eye—trying to avoid these land mines is nearly impossible.

THE CRIMINAL

So it's not like he was a hard-core felon. I'm not really into hard-core anything (except maybe for some extreme shoe and handbag shopping). He didn't murder anyone; he just screwed people out of millions of dollars. I mean, find me a wealthy man in Los Angeles who hasn't done that, right? He was just one of the unlucky bastards who got caught.

Okay, fine . . . so he was also charged with possibly assaulting his ex-girlfriend, but she eventually dropped the charges. Who hasn't gotten into some pretty nutty, alcohol-induced fights with a boyfriend or girlfriend—am I right? Plus, I'm all for second chances. Oh, and he had his own plane. #LoveAtFirstFlight. I much prefer dating men who have private air travel at their disposal, but in my defense, I did also date a guy with a roommate and a bus pass. I'm an equal-opportunist, but who doesn't like to go VIP?

We met one fateful night at my absolute favorite watering hole and home away from home, the Polo Lounge in the Beverly Hills Hotel. I was enjoying a girls' night out and hoping there might be some nice male eye candy. I thought the dating gods were finally throwing me a bone when I saw this guy who was handsome in that silver fox, John Slattery from *Mad Men,* kind of way. We kept locking eyes across the room, and I couldn't help but notice the petite young brunette superglued to his side. Usually, I would *never* go after another woman's man, but he wasn't wearing a wedding ring (or sporting a ring tan line) and she couldn't have been more than six years old, so I figured it wasn't a romantic type of situation. I finally offered him a small, sly smile while twisting my hair, and he quickly approached our table.

"My daughter wanted to meet the pretty blonde," he said through a wide smile.

Okay, that should have been my first sign that he was a little slimy. Who uses their kids to pick up dates? I mean, I can wrap my head around using your dog or even a nephew or a niece, but not your own child. He was lucky I was already feeling my second glass of Whispering Angel, so I overlooked the comment and allowed him—and his daughter—to slide into my booth. (No, that's not a sexual reference. Gross.)

"You're a terrible parent." It was the first thing I whispered to him. He was visibly taken aback. (I'm a firm believer that certain guys love to be insulted. The big, powerful types who have people kiss their asses all day long find it refreshing when a girl calls them on their shit.)

"Excuse me?" he said, through the hint of a smile.

"You're a terrible parent," I repeated a little more loudly, but not enough for his daughter—who was already focused on a video game—to hear. "It's eleven P.M. and your daughter is still awake on a weeknight . . . while you're out drinking. Shouldn't she have been in bed hours ago?"

He stumbled through some story about jet lag and a long, late afternoon nap. He could tell I wasn't buying it when I stopped paying attention about halfway through. I have two kids and knew it was a total bullshit excuse. He could see my interest was fading.

"Can I get you another drink?" he asked.

"Sure," I said, with a shrug. With the snap of his fingers, a waiter emerged with a bottle of Whispering Angel and three fresh wineglasses. (Did I mention I was at the hotel with one of my best friends, who also happens to be the coauthor of this book and my first one? You don't think I hang out at bars by myself, do you? #NotYet Anyway.) We engaged in what most people considered harmless small talk, but the rules aren't quite the same in Los Angeles. It's a choreographed dance, and every question had to be spot on.

"Where do you live?" he asked.

Okay, I thought. *I got this one.*

"Right off Mulholland," I said. My answer was specific enough that it wouldn't appear I was avoiding the question, but vague enough that I could have been a billionaire or a single mom with a two-bedroom rental house in Encino.

"Where's your home?" I asked, taking a sip of wine.

He smiled and, without missing a beat, said, "Oh, I'm constantly shuttling between L.A. and San Jose. No place really feels like home."

Point, Silver Fox. He was able to use my words to craft an even more vague response while still seeming forthright. Okay, maybe it was expensive wine goggles or the way he expertly returned my serve, but he was looking *really* attractive. I had to regain control of the conversation quickly: "How interesting. What is it that you do?"

His icy blue eyes flashed. It was on.

"I'm a venture capitalist," he replied through a toothy grin (translation: I'm filthy rich but don't actually work). I continued looking at him. If you acknowledge the response, he no longer feels obligated to continue. So I didn't. He finally relented: "I've invested with some high-profile start-ups in Silicon Valley." He took a sip of his wine. "And you?"

"And me what?" I said, pretending to play dumb.

"What do *you* do?"

"Ah," I purred. Since joining *Housewives*, this has been a very tricky question for me. If I tell men that I'm currently appearing on a very popular reality show, it usually has one of two reactions: (a) it sends them sprinting to the nearest exit as soon as the words cross my lips, or (b) it encourages them to pursue me even harder, because this could be their fifteen minutes in the spotlight. I had yet to meet the man who just wanted Brandi.

"I'm a writer, of course."

Point, Brandi.

We continued our playful back-and-forth for a few more minutes, before I abruptly (always keep them wanting more!) turned my attention to the tiny brunette next to me on her iPhone—of course she had her own cell phone. I asked if I could watch her play Angry Birds.

"It's called Tiny Wings," she gently corrected. I watched as her tired eyes bounced *all over* the screen following a little blue bird racing up and down hills. I could feel the Silver Fox watching us intently.

"She really should be sleeping," I said. Without hesitation, he motioned to a large man in a black suit to come to our table. His security, I figured.

"Please take her out to the car," the Silver Fox said, before turning his attention to his daughter. "Come on, baby, time to put on your jacket." She scooted out of the booth and struggled to pull on her brown fluffy fur jacket, which I assumed had to be real. After all, this was Beverly Hills. The security guard scooped the little girl up in his arms, her white leggings dangling over his stomach, and disappeared into the lobby.

"Well, Brandi," he said slowly and purposefully while signing a check that seemed to magically appear on the table. "It was lovely meeting you."

He looked up and smiled. My response here was crucial. It would determine if I was the type of girl you take to dinner or the type of girl you take to a hotel room. While I'm definitely a "take to a nice restaurant" kind of girl, after a few nice dinners I could definitely get down with the hotel room thing too.

I met his gaze and said, "You get that little girl to bed now."

Nailed it.

He gave me a wink (which should have been yet another clue to just how cheesy he was) and put his wallet in his jacket pocket. He made his way to the doorway but not before stopping to shake hands with at least three different people during the fifteen-foot walk.

My girlfriend had long since checked out of our conversation and was talking to a group of people at the bar, but she rejoined me as soon as he slunk away. We topped off our glasses with what was left of the wine, and I waited. This was the cat-and-mouse game I had missed: the innuendos, the seduction, the saying nothing with your mouth and everything with your eyes. I had been with an older man before, but there was something incredibly sexy about this one.

Not five minutes had passed before he emerged again in the doorway. He marched straight to my table, ignoring the hoots of the people he knew at neighboring tables, and said, "I'd like to take you to dinner."

I smiled and crossed my arm into my lap.

"Can I give you my number?" he asked.

It was a power move that would in theory give me control but ultimately would force *me* to call *him*. Then, if I didn't call, he could pretend he wasn't even interested enough to get my number, and if I did, he could brag about how much I must want him if I was calling. I knew this game. I've played this game.

"My phone is dead," I shrugged. That's right, I was actually going to make him ask for my number. He let out a small laugh.

Point, Brandi.

When I got back to my house after midnight, I plugged my phone in to charge and found that I had five text messages from my girlfriend who I had just left. I scrolled through and read one after the other:

"Oh my god. He went to jail!"

"He served like actual time. OMG!"

"Shit. He's like a legit white collar sleazeball."

"He squandered millions of dollars."

"It was in every newspaper!"

This particular friend was well versed in researching and finding people online, so as soon as she got home she started googling the shit out of this guy. What are friends for, right?

"Calm down," I texted. "Who in L.A. hasn't spent time in jail?" I was a little buzzed and getting ready for bed. "Let's chat in the A.M." I would do my own online research in the morning, but right then I had a date with my pillow that I just couldn't miss.

After I scrubbed my face and applied my absolute favorite EMK Placental mask, I heard the pings on my phone start coming through one after the other.

"You can't go out with him!"

"I'm not kidding. He was charged with assaulting his ex-girlfriend!"

"She had to get a restraining order. She says she was terrified for her life!"

"Terrified. For. Her. L-I-F-E!!!!"

"He's a crazy person. He'll chop you up into little bitty pieces and leave your body scattered throughout garbage bins in The Valley!"

Clearly my girlfriend was being a little dramatic, but yes, this was definitely alarming and something I wouldn't take lightly. Regardless of circumstances, men should *never* lay a finger on a woman. In a woman? Yes. On a woman? No. I promised her that I would be okay for the night (it's not like he had my home address) and that we'd talk about it in the morning.

By nine A.M., the Criminal had already left me a voice mail. When I finally crawled out of bed, relishing one of those rare mornings I got to sleep in, I poured myself a cup of coffee with my vanilla Coffee-mate creamer and called my girlfriend. Immediately, she pulled up an article online recounting how he had convinced his business partners to invest in a doomed tech company but somehow managed to pocket millions for himself before he and the business went belly-up. Apparently, he partied pretty hard and developed a wicked cocaine addiction. He also had a well-documented, acrimonious breakup with the mother of that adorable little six-year-old. The mother later claimed he assaulted her and filed for a restraining order. That was not the only time he was arrested. #Ugh.

I know all too well that the public spotlight isn't always favorable, especially when the media latches on to a really juicy story. This, however, was a little too intense . . . even for me. Or was it? Aren't there two sides to every story? That's what they tell me anyway.

"Don't even call him back. He may go all *Fatal Attraction* on you," my friend said.

At that point, I wasn't planning on seeing him again, but for some reason I felt compelled to at least hear him out. There were plenty of people who had never given me the opportunity to tell my side of the story, so I figured I owed him that.

I went about my day as usual, deciding that I would return his call that evening. I debated getting it over with that morning, but just because we weren't going to be sparring anymore doesn't mean you give up on the game.

It turned out I didn't have to worry about it. He called again after lunch. #StalkMuch?

"Hi," I said, answering the phone with a knowing tone.

"Hi," he said back, his voice matching mine.

I'm not one for beating around the bush, so I jumped right into it.

"There are some pretty major omissions from your story last night."

I've always been blunt and honest. He's an adult; I'm an adult. Unless it's a form of foreplay, why waste our time tiptoeing around the actual conversation?

"I figured you did some recon, which is why I'm calling again," he replied. I could hear that he was no longer smiling when he spoke to me. "Look, there are two sides to every story. I really like you, so I just ask that you listen to mine."

I imagine this conversation wasn't foreign to him. It's common practice to google someone before you date him or her (as discussed in chapter 10), so he probably had this monologue memorized. Listen, this guy wasn't stupid. He proceeded to tell me first that he was the scapegoat for a massive company-wide error but took it on the chin because ultimately he was the point guy. If someone was going to fall, it had to be him. Plus, he knew that if he ever wanted to work again, he'd have to do penance and have a few Silicon Valley bigwigs "owe" him afterward. He openly admitted that he got caught up in the drug scene but had been free of anything illegal for more than two years. (Who could fault the guy for being on Lexapro? I was on it after one night in Beverly Hills prison.) Finally, he said, the assault charges were dropped—as was the restraining order. His ex-girlfriend was apparently bat-shit crazy (I have yet to meet a guy who hasn't referred to an ex as "crazy"), and he now had sole custody of their daughter because of this.

"If a judge thought I was even the smallest threat to my daughter, would he have ever placed her in my care?" he asked me.

I sat silent for a few moments taking this all in. It sounded plausible, right? I mean, who would put this much time into an elaborate lie just so he could get laid? Plus, I was supposed to be dating again . . . wasn't I? Given the guys in Los Angeles, this wasn't *that* much baggage. Or so I thought.

"Look, I'm not saying we get married tomorrow. I'm just saying have dinner with me," he pleaded sweetly, before adding: "I still want to go out with you even though I'm *only* 50 percent sure you won't slash the tires of my car."

I couldn't help but laugh. Clearly, he had done his research too. I decided to take him at his word because he sounded incredibly sincere.

"I'm headed up to San Jose tonight, but I'm hoping to

be wheels up by four P.M. tomorrow," he said. "If you decide to take a chance, I can come scoop you up on my way into town from Van Nuys."

Wheels up? I thought. The expression wasn't lost on me. Plus, the only planes that land in or take off out of Van Nuys Airport are private ones, but I wasn't going to give him the satisfaction of acknowledging this.

"Fine," I said. "I'll go out with you, but I'll meet you at the restaurant at eight. Could you please send your driver for me." Sure, I was being bossy, but that's what he got for pulling the "Van Nuys" card. If you're going to throw around how much money you have to impress a woman, you can't get pissed when she requests certain luxuries.

I have a rule about always meeting on neutral territory for a first date. He was a criminal after all! Sure, I chose to believe his side of the story, but I wasn't trying to tempt fate either.

"Where should we go?" he asked.

Ugh. This is my biggest pet peeve. Listen up, guys. If you're going to ask someone out on a fucking date, *take them on a fucking date.* I understand that you may want to be sensitive to your date's preferences, but I don't find anything more unattractive than a guy who can't make up his mind. Be a man. Take me on a date. Go on fucking Yelp if you need to, but don't ask me for suggestions.

He finally decided that we would go to Madeo—a

fancy Italian restaurant that's a West Hollywood institution. I'm a *huge* pasta lover, and it happened to be one of my favorite restaurants. Plus, I had known the maître d' for years, so it made me feel a little safer just in case the Criminal was totally psycho.

When I arrived at the restaurant, it actually took me a moment to recognize him. I guess I didn't realize how tipsy I was when we met. *Hmm*, I thought. He wasn't as attractive as I remembered—stupid fucking wine goggles. After a thirty-minute wait at the bar, we were shoved into a corner table in the "bistro" section of the restaurant (translation: no-man's-land). I started questioning if he was really as powerful and important as he wanted me to believe. Besides all of that—and his incessant need to call me "baby" on our first date, my least favorite pet name of all time—the date went surprisingly . . . okay. He walked me to the town car that he had waiting and asked if he could see me again. "Sure," I said. He went in for a kiss, but I turned my head in time and leaned in for a hug.

A few days later, I invited the Criminal to my friend's art show in downtown L.A. He was very vocal about being Mr. MoneyBags, so I figured he might want to invest in a few of her pieces. When the Criminal finally arrived, it was like someone let the Tasmanian Devil out of his cage. He buzzed around the room at warp speed in a really bad rainbow neck scarf that I fucking hated, trading business cards with anybody who would give him the time of day. Every so often, he would pop over to where I was standing with friends, give me an aggressive squeeze, and call me "baby" at least three times. My book agent—or as I lovingly call him, my gaygent— pulled the Criminal to the side and let him have it. "You're cracked out of your head running around this room, and you're a felon! Stay away from Brandi!" he shouted, then huffed off. What can I say? My gaygent may lack tact, but he loves me hard. Maybe it was time I started listening to him.

When I went to check in with the Criminal, he seemed unfazed by his scolding and said, "There's this party we *have* to go to after dinner. It's going to be epic." Before I could even answer, he went back to making rounds.

"Am I imagining things, or is he on drugs?" I asked my friend Asher, who was standing with me.

"Oh, he's definitely coked up," he said with a laugh. "That guy is hilarious."

I decided not to share with Asher that the Criminal had supposedly been "drug free" for two years. After the art show, I invited Asher along to dinner with the Criminal and me. There is safety in numbers.

"Isn't that a little awkward?" Asher asked. "Aren't you supposed to be on a date?"

"You are not fucking leaving me alone with him," I spit at him through gritted teeth.

For dinner, we decided to return to the scene of the crime: the Beverly Hills Hotel. The Criminal was bouncing from one conversation to the next, stopping every few minutes to greet someone else he knew in the restaurant.

"You guys are coming to this party, right?" he asked Asher and me at least four times. I had avoided answering the question. Could this really be the same guy who I met here just a week earlier? Was I that drunk the first night? Or was he just that coked up now? He was acting like a psycho. After we finished eating—and downed a few cocktails—he invited two very attractive lesbians from the bar to sit with us.

Was he fucking kidding me? We were supposed to be on a date.

Sure, I brought Asher along, but that was purely for security reasons. He was actually hitting on these women right in front of me. I had zero doubt that he would have gone upstairs with all three of us that very minute if I gave him the impression that it was something I'd be into.

So I told him as much, and he said, "Baby, you're being crazy. I'm just giving them a hard time. Take it easy, baby."

The last time a man told me that I was being "crazy" for believing something I witnessed before my very eyes, I ended up in the middle of a tabloid cheating scandal. *Fuck that*, I thought. I excused myself to use the ladies' room but heard him come into the bathroom a minute later.

"Baby, are you okay?" he asked.

Oh my God, I thought. Did he seriously just walk into the women's bathroom?

"Yeah, dude," I said. "I'm just using the bathroom."

"Okay," he said, "but hurry up. We have to get to this party."

I texted my friend Asher from the stall and said we needed a fucking exit plan. Not only did I have zero interest in going to this party, if I had to hear about it one more fucking time I was going to lose it. When I returned to the table, Asher had already picked up the check. #True Gentleman.

"I think I'm gonna call it for tonight," I told the Criminal, barely covering my annoyance.

"You have to come! It's supposed to be epic," he said, and here came the point of no return: "It's at Brendan Fraser's condo."

There were *so* many things wrong with what he said. Perhaps I would have jumped all over the opportunity to go party with Encino Man if this were fucking 1995. In 2013, it's just not fucking happening. Really? This was the party he had been going on and on about. To be fair, I've got nothing against Brendan Fraser, but the Criminal was talking about it like we just got invited to Clooney's house on Lake fucking Como. But no, he was talking about some actor who probably *actually* lived in Encino at this point . . . in a rental. Like myself.

The next morning, I woke up to a barrage of texts from the Criminal rattling on about the "epic" Brendan Fraser party. We didn't see each other again after that night, and I stopped returning his texts.

It's funny that in the end it wasn't his shady history that came between us, his poor parenting skills, or even the fact that he wasn't as fabulous as he let on. It was Brendan Fraser.

THE DIVORCÉ

I immediately knew I liked him. He felt somehow safe.

We hadn't actually met yet, but we both knew of one another.

He had two kids approximately the same age as my boys and, like me, recently went through a pretty turbulent divorce. We had about a dozen mutual friends, so his name was constantly popping up on my Facebook feed—and we were constantly responding to one another's witty comments on photos and posts.

This felt so much easier than meeting a strange guy at the Polo Lounge or in a grocery store parking lot. I had great friends, so if he was close with them too, it must mean he was a decent guy. He was really cute according to his profile photo, and I remember seeing his name once linked to a very high-profile actress a few years back.

After a few weeks of the Facebook flirting, he finally sent me a message with his phone number. I remember thinking it was a pretty ballsy move coming from a guy I didn't really know, but I liked it. So I shot him a simple text saying: "Now you have my number too." I wasn't going to actually call a complete stranger, but I was proud of myself for taking this first step. The old Brandi would have shut down all communication once it got "real," but I was taking steps to open myself up again. He called me later that day and asked me out to dinner. I almost surprised myself when I immediately agreed.

He was a handsome Jewish born-and-bred Los Angeles native with a biting sense of humor that I just adored. But I quickly learned that as a recently divorced man, he had plenty of oats left to sow. I considered cutting it off before it really even got going because a guy who has spent years sleeping with the same woman would undoubtedly have a wandering eye.

No, Brandi, I thought. *You're going to see this one through.*

While my gut told me to run, I knew I had to give him a chance. It was all a part of this new journey, I told myself. We probably wouldn't end up riding off into the sunset, but I needed to get my feet wet dating again (and, perhaps, not just my feet).

After a few casual dates, the Divorcé invited me to Napa for the weekend. It seemed really soon for such a romantic wine country getaway, so I told him that it might be a little much for me. He suggested that he bring one of his single guy friends and I bring one of my single girlfriends, so it would take the pressure off. It would be more like a group trip, he explained. Clearly this guy was eager to get up my skirt, but I do love wine so how could I refuse? When my girlfriend and I arrived at Van Nuys Airport (like I said, I'm a total sucker for private planes), it immediately turned awkward. His single guy friend had brought a date for the weekend. My girlfriend shot me a look that could have pierced the skin. She was about to become the fifth wheel on this very uncomfortable weekend retreat. I promised her that we'd spend the weekend getting spa treatments and drinking great wine, because the Divorcé had an amazing hookup at this five-star resort. She finally agreed.

Despite the initial awkwardness, the Divorcé and I had a great time in Napa. It was like an episode of *The Bachelor:* put us together on a magical island with no one else around (just a dozen cameras and 7 million pairs of eyes), no responsibilities, and no real consequences, and we were perfect. But in the real world, we just weren't going to work. It felt wrong—and I could tell we were looking for different things out of our relationship (maybe it was because of the looks he kept shooting my girlfriend).

He had a constant need to prove to me—and I'm sure himself—that despite his brutal divorce (which left him sharing custody of his young children), he was still hot shit. Sure, I'm perpetually young at heart, but I don't think he wanted to accept that he was in his midforties, had a glaring bald spot, and a tendency to check out every other hot ass that entered the room. Down the road I would learn he also had an incredibly small penis. Okay, so maybe it wasn't his lack of maturity; maybe it was just the penis. But in his defense, he did make up for it a little by being an amazing kisser and ultimately became a really great friend. It was just never going to be love.

I have to say, I was proud of myself for giving him a chance. It didn't work out, but guess what? I was totally fine with it. Maybe this was the kind of stepping-stone I needed. We stopped seeing each other shortly after Napa. A few months later, I ran into him and his new girlfriend at a mutual friend's birthday party—and they were both totally into me. The Divorcé invited me to join them for an after-party at someone's home in the Hollywood Hills. Did I look like I wanted to go to some party with a bunch of twenty-somethings? That hadn't been my scene since before I got married, but he obviously was making up for lost time. For weeks after, they kept pursuing me for a threesome. Look, I'm all for some fun, sexy spontaneity, but only when I'm in the number one position. Playing the third wheel in their playtime was just not my idea of fun. I realized that while I wanted a man who had shown himself capable of commitment in the past, I needed to make sure he wasn't now making up for lost time.

Brandi's

MAYBE IT'S ABOUT TIME TO START FLYING COMMERCIAL.

Tweet-ism

4

So I Fucked a
Movie Star

STAR-FUCKER (NOUN)

Someone who sleeps with another person solely for the fact that he or she is in the public eye and is hoping to get some sort of notoriety (or pregnant) from it.

Example: The nerdy, suddenly famous actor, who never got laid in high school, now had his choice of star-fuckers, otherwise known as "cocktail mattresses."

I hate the word celebrity. *What does it really mean?* Nothing. It's just a label some blogger or tabloid plugs into a headline when photographers snap pictures of a boob falling out of your dress. Everything about it feels so self-indulgent—and I was a model. Since *Housewives,* I've occasionally been referred to as one, but I'm really just a reality personality (translation: a more sensationalized version of myself) with a severe case of foot-in-mouth syndrome. Meryl Streep, Madonna, Sean Penn—those are *real* celebrities.

Just like most people, I find myself completely starstruck whenever I meet a legitimate movie star or rock legend. Living in Los Angeles, I'm never impressed by the "I'm an actor" line. Guess what? Every waiter and bartender in L.A. is an "actor." It's like, show me your IMDb and then get back to folding napkins, because your shift starts in five minutes. After twenty years in the city, I consider myself a tried-and-true Angeleno (it's rare to meet an *actual* native). During my years in LaLa Land, I have known my fair share of "famous" people and even had the pleasure of brunching on occasion with Hollywood legend Bruce Willis (#DieHard), but even so, I still have a hard time playing it cool when someone like Johnny Depp walks into a restaurant.

When it comes to my dating life, I *try* to stay as far away from the "celebrity" pool as possible. It's nothing but trouble. Trust me, I've been there and done that. But I was trying to keep an open mind—and it's hard to avoid actors in L.A., especially the good-looking ones.

I didn't always have a "just say no to actors" policy. Only after I divorced one.

Shortly after moving to West Hollywood, my stunning roommate Michelle and I were at the Whiskey Bar inside the Sunset Marquis Hotel. On any given night, it was a who's who of Hollywood's hottest actors, musicians, and socialites mixed with some movie execs, high-profile investors, and model-types. On one particular evening, I was introduced to an up-and-coming comedian (let's call him Danny). I immediately recognized him from some bit movie parts here and there, but he wasn't a household name . . . yet. He had the kind of face you remember—sharp features, thick dark hair, and a goofy grin. He bought me a drink, and we spent the next few hours talking and laughing. His particular brand of sarcasm and wit was sexy. I am a sucker for a guy with a great sense of humor, so even though I had about six inches of height on Danny, I found myself surprisingly and wildly attracted to him. Before leaving, he asked for my number and said he would love to have dinner some time.

He called about a week later and asked if I wanted to come over to his place for dinner and a movie (clearly this was code for dinner and sex). His house was one of those bachelor pads set high in the Hollywood Hills overlooking the city lights. It was beautiful, but clearly decorated by someone other than himself (#ExGirlfriendAlert). We laughed so hard that night that my stomach was hurting and my jaw was sore (it sometimes ends up sore after a date, but not from giggling). There was a natural rhythm to our conversation that made us both feel comfortable with each other. It only turned awkward when I asked him why he still had photos of his ex-girlfriend (now a well-known actress) everywhere. He mumbled something and immediately changed the subject.

When he finally decided that it was time to turn up the heat, we started making out on the couch. Something about me towering over the guy while sitting upright was strange, so he suggested we take things to the bedroom. Perhaps if we were lying down, he'd be more at ease.

Despite his height, I was impressed with the size of his manhood. I mean, it wasn't "holy shit" big, but it was a respectable size for a guy who was maybe five feet seven. This is where things got awkward again. We had spent the evening laughing so much that I couldn't stop laughing when it was time to get serious. Every time I looked at him, I'd think of something funny he said or remember one of his characters and would burst into hysterics. It didn't help the mood. When I regained my composure, we'd get back to it. He'd look deeply into my eyes, with an expression so serious it felt like a joke, so I started cracking up again. This wasn't making the mood very sexy, but I eventually was able to control my manic giggling and enjoyed the evening. We saw each other a few more times over the next month, but I couldn't help but feel I was hanging out with a really good friend and not a potential love interest. After all, I couldn't really fall for a guy who would make me laugh instead of come.

When I first met my ex-husband, I was casually dating one of the biggest television stars of the nineties (let's call him Andrew).

I met him in August 1995 at the Whiskey Bar, naturally. Like most drama geeks, Andrew had a lot of fucking to do to make up for his nerdy high school years, so he was out chasing skirts with another actor (let's call him Larry). Almost immediately after Michelle and I arrived, these two guys waved us over to the booth where they were holding court. Like his character, Andrew was charming and funny—in a quirky kind of way—but Michelle had already connected with him, and I was more interested in his better-looking, less-charismatic friend anyhow. (I mean, of course I go for the stupidest, hottest guy in the room. Typical Brandi move.) I didn't really give Andrew another thought until about two weeks later. He had taken Michelle out on a disastrous first date and called her a few days later to say hello. Michelle and I shared an apartment—this one had a land line. She wasn't home at the time—and totally not interested in seeing him again—so he and I shot the shit for a few minutes, and he proceeded to ask *me* to dinner. Let the record show that I am a firm believer in the golden rule of any female friendship: keep your friends close and their exes really fucking far away. So I declined—because that's what friends do—even though I knew Michelle had already become hot and heavy with a commercial director who was feeding her a ton of work. #$$$$. I mentioned to her that Andrew had called looking for her and we actually had a great conversation. Michelle suggested to me that I should go out with him, because she couldn't possibly care less. So when he called a week later (#BoysAlwaysDo), I told him I'd love to go to dinner.

As a twenty-three-year-old girl, I found the sex to be pretty standard—which means it *never* would have cut it at thirty or forty. #ForgetAboutIt. But he overcompensated for his lack of bedroom expertise with an incredible appetite for eating pussy (which I can appreciate even more now, because going downtown seems to be a rarity for many men I've dated). His schedule was insane, but we got together whenever he had time away from shooting. He was still reeling from a pretty devastating breakup with a beautiful musician (#Obsessed), and we both knew I was just his twenty-something rebound girl with a cute ass. Honestly, I enjoyed being his L.A. arm candy. It's funny, because as much as we went out, you'll never find a photo of us. Things were so much more undercover in those days without all the paparazzi, blogs, and tabloids. Andrew's level of celebrity at the time put him at the top of every exclusive guest list. There wasn't a velvet rope that didn't part for him upon arrival or a reservation at the hottest restaurant that wasn't immediately made available. Imagine the Red Sea, but instead of water parting it was an ocean of Von Dutch trucker hats. I had traveled all over the world at that point, but there's something about being a part of the Hollywood in-crowd that's completely intoxicating. But like many actors, he wasn't immune to drinking his own brand of douche-y Kool-Aid, so I had begun to pull away. We were never exclusive, and his dinner invites had started to become fewer and farther between, so when I locked eyes with my ex-husband for the first time one fateful night at the Hollywood nightclub Granville, I didn't hesitate to move the fuck on (and quickly). Like I said, Andrew was just using me. He had girls in every city—and, in his eyes, we girls were a dime a dozen. But I quickly learned that "celebrities" don't like being rejected.

As soon as I started declining his date night invitations and stopped returning his calls altogether, his demeanor seemed to get more aggressive. It was clear that this man wasn't used to the word "no" anymore. (Maybe it stirred up those old memories of high school rejection. Did his prom date stand him up or something?) He could have easily moved on to just about any hot girl in Hollywood, but he wouldn't quit pursuing me. His messages got more and more intense, and by "messages" I mean voice recordings on my old-school answering machine where pushing play would allow the roomful of people to hear the eleven voice mails he had left (welcome to the nineties, bitches!).

The messages started out arrogant, but soon became kind of sweet, then started to get overly angry and then finally apologetic, pathetic, and just bat-shit crazy. It's like, dude, I'm sorry no one fucked you until you got famous, but leave me the hell alone! He eventually figured out that I was dating a ridiculously good-looking but little-known soap opera actor, so he had his agent reach out to my ex-husband's manager, knowing damn well it would probably be the biggest casting call of my ex-husband's career. Apparently, Andrew couldn't handle a less successful, more attractive man dating me, so his agent invited my ex and his manager to dinner. What was he hoping to achieve with this incredibly awkward meeting? Was he going to talk him out of dating me? Was he going to beg him to step aside? I guess we'll never know, because my ex declined the invitation because I had asked him to—and he had already pledged his undying devotion to me. (Something he made a habit of during our thirteen years together. #Lesson Learned.) Looking back, I might have had a bigger divorce settlement had I stuck it out with Andrew and followed my head instead of my heart, but I wouldn't have ended up creating the two most insanely amazing little boys in the world. It's been a while since I've seen Andrew, but we occasionally bump into each other around town. We're always polite, exchange pleasantries, but never speak of the past. And perhaps he's just a wee bit anxious I still have those messages. It wouldn't be the first time I saved a recording. #DrinkingAndTweeting.

After my divorce, I swore up and down that I would never date another actor. Besides my best friend, who married the most amazing, incredibly kind superstar ever, I haven't witnessed many actor relationships that have been both healthy and long-lasting.

I like to think I was somewhat successful in keeping that promise to myself, because since my divorce I've only dated a couple of actors (but they were all totally by accident, I swear). #Hypocrite. I rationalized my decision, because celebrities are really no different than anyone else—they put their pants on one leg at a time and have the same number of hours in the day to get their shit done. They're just like you and me but have worked hard (or bedded enough producers) to become successful in their careers. Even a superstar like George Clooney has everyday problems like needing LASIK eye surgery to correct his vision. (Side note: George Clooney is a pretty great guy and one of the few movie stars who are down-to-earth and charming. I've met him through my ex-boyfriend. Isn't he single again?)

Most actors are, however, extremely self-serving and think you should consider yourself lucky because they've given you the opportunity to fuck a celebrity. I find that dating one usually ends up badly, so unless you're getting a free trip to the Cannes Film Festival, I'd steer clear. But like I've said countless times: do as I say and not as I do.

First, I'll tell you about the action hero.

The sky was a pinkish orange as the sun began dipping below the Pacific Ocean. If I had had a phone handy, I probably would have tweeted it. #Not. I was on the beach playing ring-around-the-rosy with a group of my friends' little girls. My boys were with their dad that night, and I honestly love being around children. (What can I say? Kids love me because I am a giant kid at heart.)

A well-known NHL player was hosting a fabulous house party at his beachfront Malibu mansion that afternoon. I had been invited in the past, but my ex-husband was never fond of me frolicking on the beach in a small bikini around professional athletes. #GoFigure. After a full day of fun in the sun and hanging out with my richest, semiwasted friends, I was preparing to go home but promised the little girls on the beach just one more game. I was even more eager to make my exit once I noticed the second wave of partygoers starting to arrive clad in full cocktail attire, while I was makeup-less in a bathing suit with a sheer cover-up and had sand *everywhere*. Plus, I noticed the new issue of *Glamour* magazine, which included a feature about me, sitting on the coffee table of the NHL player's house, and all I wanted to do was snag the copy, go home, and crawl into bed with it. Honestly, I was eager to see what spewed out of my mouth this time in my favorite glossy.

I was making my fifth lap around the "rosy" with all the kids when I heard loud laughter and shouts coming from the house as more people poured in. Most of the daytime partygoers had left, but a giant bus had just unleashed a gaggle of very attractive girls dressed in "evening bikinis," full makeup, and six-inch stilettos. #WhoreDeliveryService. I looked over my shoulder right before my newest little girlfriends and I dropped to the sand and spotted two very famous actors making their way through the crowds, complete with bro hugs, air kisses, and high fives. The rich and famous love Malibu's premiere beachfront row—as do the star-fuckers. #NotMe. #BeenThere. #DoneThat. These are gorgeous, roughly four-thousand-square-feet homes that overlook the Pacific Ocean. These coveted abodes sell for way over $20 million. The more cost-effective approach is to rent one for a month in the summer, if you have an extra $200,000 lying around. That's why these high-profile types love to live there. It's exclusive, only very few people can afford to live there, and it's not super-easy to get to, so tourists usually opt for the Hollywood Walk of Fame and the Santa Monica Pier for sightseeing (think: fanny packs, cameras, and Hawaiian shirts). But Malibu is still close enough to Los Angeles, so if you choose to leave this luxurious little town, you can be anywhere within the hour.

I turned my attention back to the action on the beach, but a few moments later I heard someone walking up behind me—it was one of the movie stars.

"Hi," he said. "I'm —." Let's call him Marty. "What's your name?"

"Brandi," I said and continued to dance in the sand. Only this time, I knew I had an admirer who was watching my every move. #KnowTheGame. Instead of playfully circling with the girls, I shimmied down the sand a bit to where some adult friends were enjoying cocktails and listening to music. I began to move my hips and shake around a little more provocatively. His eyes never left me—and I knew it. It was starting to get uncomfortable. Okay, not really. I loved it.

"I'm headed to the Malibu Beach Inn," he said, approaching me from behind. "Do you wanna join me?"

So slick, I thought.

"No, I really can't," I purred. A smile crept across his

face; he seemed amused by my rejection. Apparently, women didn't usually deny his advances, but I already had plans for the evening—nothing he could offer me was better than cuddling up with my pups and my favorite fashion magazine. Plus, like I said, I wasn't wearing any makeup and I was all too familiar with the lighting situation at that specific "inn." I wasn't interested in exposing myself . . . in that way. While I wasn't interested in heading home with him that night, that wasn't to say I wasn't interested in a possible future date. Plus, playing hard to get is like the first lesson mothers should teach their daughters. The more available you are, the less interesting you are. #Fact.

"Could I get your number?" he asked after a long pause.

"Sure," I said coyly. I waited for him to produce a phone or, at the very least, a pen. I mean, I wasn't above writing my number on his palm. Whoever he ended up going home with that night might have ended up with a "Brandi brand" on her ass. #GetIt?

"Go ahead," he said.

"There's no way you're going to remember it," I said.

"Try me," he said.

The next morning I woke to a text message from Marty asking what my plans were for the afternoon. At first I was totally floored that he remembered my number, but I suppose for actors, memorizing shit is part of the job requirement. I considered my day, and I was unusually flexible (figuratively and literally—Pilates really does work wonders). The boys were with their dad, so besides the normal errands—Sephora, Target, and maybe a manicure—I had the day free. I responded that my afternoon was open but I had dinner plans and needed to be home by five P.M. He didn't need to know that I was really just pretending. You never want to seem too available. #BeAChallenge.

"Would you like to grab lunch?" he texted back after a few minutes. It was clear that he was eager to see me and wouldn't back down easily.

Fuck, I thought. *Why not?* After all, "yes is my new no!"

It was after one P.M. when I finally arrived at his beachside residence with floor-to-ceiling windows and a view of the Pacific. It was a "come fuck me" house that I'm sure worked just about every time. I had spent hours perfecting my impossibly natural not-wearing-makeup makeup look and opted for an itsy-bitsy bikini and a semi-sheer cover-up. I was going for the "I wasn't trying" look. By the time I made my way to his front door, my stomach was in knots. Marty answered the door in shorts and a T-shirt and invited me inside. He seemed super-jumpy, so that immediately put me on edge. This wasn't off to a great start. He gave me the grand tour of his pristinely decorated summer rental home, but strangely paused before each of the twelve floor-to-ceiling windows and peeked to see if there were any photographers lingering outside. With each window he passed, he pulled closed the curtain and continued the tour. I was pretty used to the paparazzi scene in Los Angeles at this point, but this kind of paranoia seemed a little over the top. I had seen countless photos of him in magazines, striding shirtless on the beach, so I never considered that he actually didn't want the attention. I began to feel incredibly uncomfortable and wasn't sure how to act. Was he nervous that someone would spot him inside his house? Or worse, was he nervous someone would spot *me*?

I was starting to get extremely insecure with this entire ordeal. When the tour finally ended, he could tell that I had tensed up and offered me a glass of wine. I wasn't planning on drinking and still had a court-mandated Breathalyzer in my car from my DUI charge the previous year that I needed to blow into before starting the engine. #DefinitelyNoDrinkingAndDriving.

"I thought you were sober," I blurted out. *Shit,* I thought. There I go again. I didn't want to offend him, but clearly I have a tendency to word-vomit. Marty looked at me and shrugged.

"I am, but I still keep wine here for when I have guests," he explained.

I accepted his offer—it seemed rude not to after that—and he ducked into the kitchen to grab me a glass. He made no mention of the lunch plans, but I don't think I could have forced myself to eat anyway. I was just too anxious at this point with all the window covering and fumbled conversation.

We spent the next two hours talking, and I finally began to relax. We talked at length about my divorce and ex-husband; he shared similar war stories of his past relationships. It became clear that he was a serial modelizer, but his honesty was refreshing and his eyes were sparkling. #SuckerForEyes. Plus, Marty had no idea who my ex-husband was, which was refreshing.

My single glass of pinot grigio kicked in, and our conversation escalated to flirting and touching. He would grab my thigh when he laughed, and I would gently push his shoulder when he playfully ribbed me. It wasn't long before we started making out. He stood up from the couch with my legs wrapped around his waist. He placed his hands under my ass and carried me to his bedroom—making out the entire way.

Why is it that the powerful, successful men you expect to be rock stars in bed rarely are? I firmly believe that there is a direct correlation between the kind of car a man drives and his ability to make you orgasm. The guy in the beat-up 1998 Honda Accord can fuck you like the world is ending, but the guy in the Bentley expects you to do all the work. Should I feel lucky that he's been in a few movies and is gracious enough to let me lie in his bed?

To be fair, he wasn't *bad* in bed. Actually, he seemed to know his way rather well around a woman, but I guess I just wasn't feeling it. A few minutes in, I knew that I needed to make my escape, so I got him to come the quickest way I knew how: enter Brandi's special sex-tastic secret magic trick.

I whispered a command in his ear and he looked at me with hungry eyes and, without saying a word, obliged.

"More," I said. I felt his heart rate accelerating and his breath quickening. Celebrity or not, guys are so fucking predictable.

Presto! He collapsed on top of me, apologizing that he came so quickly. #ThankGodForCondoms.

There's something my special little trick does that pushes men over the edge. Don't ask me why, but it works . . . every time. You may want to know what it is, but it wouldn't be my secret little sex trick if everyone knew . . . now would it?

"It was amazing for me too," I purred.

I quickly dressed and pulled the old "Will you look at the time?" line. Like I've said, I'm a terrible liar and needed to get out of there as soon as possible. I thanked him for a lovely afternoon before scooting out the door. I jumped into my car and blew into the Breathalyzer, but the engine wouldn't start.

Fuck. And this "fuck" was not like the one I just had.

With my tail between my legs, I walked back to his door.

"Forget something?" he asked. I explained, with extreme embarrassment, that my car wouldn't start because of my "situation."

"Let me get you a water," he suggested, opening the hulking metal door just enough for me to slide back in. I could sense a faint hint of satisfaction in his voice. He returned with a large glass and announced that he was actually about to head out to a party, but that I was more than welcome to stay while I "sobered up." Just like that, the ball was back in his court.

For being so paranoid, I thought it was odd that he just let me sit in his house. I sat on the couch for an hour and flipped through magazines before trying to start my car again. Luckily, it worked this time. Seriously, it was one glass of wine like four hours earlier. #Lightweight.

A few days later, Marty called to ask if I wanted to grab lunch. I agreed but said I would meet him at the restaurant. I knew that I wasn't interested in sleeping with him, but maybe if we spent more time together that would change. I'm all for second chances, and after confiding in a few ecstatic girlfriends that I had "casually hooked up with this movie star," I decided I'd be silly not to give him another shot.

It was fun while it lasted, but the sparks just weren't there. And I was certain they never would be. . . . The rest is TMZ history.

Next, there was the actor/rapper/political hopeful.

He was the most gorgeous man I'd ever seen: tall, dark, and handsome with milk chocolate skin, luscious lips, and the sort of chiseled abs you could see through his T-shirt.

When I first spotted him, I was doing what all the cool kids do in West Hollywood, grabbing a drink at a local members-only club, with my young, hot artist friend Cari. I immediately recognized him from one of my favorite TV shows. He was sitting in one of the club's leather-covered circular booths facing the bar, but he couldn't stop glancing over in my direction. After an hour of catching each other's eye—and a few well-timed, back arches and head tilts on my part—he crossed the four feet from his table to the bar. I saw him heading my way, so I did what any girl would do in my position: I pretended to be in a riveting conversation with my girlfriend. He was going to have to wait if he wanted to get my attention . . . or so I wanted him to think. I felt him saddle up on the bar stool next to me, but I was turned in the opposite direction. When I finally angled myself toward the bar to reach for my glass of wine, he took the opportunity to introduce himself (let's call him Wade). I'm not one to stroke egos, but I admitted that I recognized him. #ISeriouslyCantLie. That clearly was the right answer, because his mouth opened to reveal the biggest, brightest smile with the most perfect teeth I've ever seen. (Hmm, maybe I should text him right now. Oh crap, I'm busy writing!) He began flattering me almost immediately.

"You're so gorgeous," he said. Clearly that was the right answer too, because I decided in that moment that we were going to be together. Of course not tonight, we had only just met. But eventually we would. #BrownSugar.

After about forty-five minutes of serious flirting (and the departure of my girlfriend, who had some fabulous party to attend in the Hollywood Hills), I excused myself momentarily to use the ladies' room; I needed to check my hair and lip gloss and reapply some concealer—yes, I still get pimples. When I emerged from the club's single-stall restroom, I was greeted by a particularly feisty pseudo-supermodel who approached me rapidly and said, "You're fucking with *my* man."

Was she kidding me? I looked right into her eyes and slowly, calmly, but sternly said, "Fuck you," exaggerating each word. Nobody talks to me that way; I don't care who the fuck you think you are.

"I think you have a super-fan here," I said once I got

back to the bar. "Some aggressive hot chick in the bathroom told me you were her man." Wade explained that they had dated a while back, but she was actually at the club with her new boyfriend.

"She's just crazy," he said.

There it was again. Why do men always refer to their exes as "crazy"? In this specific situation it seemed to actually be true. Either way, I didn't need the drama, so I left—but not before giving him my digits.

We began texting—and a little bit of dirty sexting—and went on a few dates before finally sleeping together. He pressed his big, soft lips to mine and would kiss me slowly and passionately. He used his huge muscles to manhandle me around the bed and made me feel tiny. He wasn't super-freaky in the sheets, but I was okay with that. It felt like making love, so I didn't even mind that his favorite position was missionary. We would kiss for the entire hour (a little too long for me, but, hey, who was I to complain?). His manhood was enormous—the perfect cherry on top of this gorgeous chocolate sundae. It was so large that he had to special-order condoms just to fit him. My seventeen-year-old kitty cat aged a few months each time we slept together—so I'm guessing she's about twenty-three now, but it was well worth it.

Wade spent most of his time traveling for work, so when he was in L.A. he stayed at a posh West Hollywood hotel. It felt like the perfect dating situation. We saw each other a few times every couple of weeks for some great conversation, great food, and great sex. He'd offer to drive all the way out to my house (I was still living in The Valley when we first started dating) to have dinner and watch movies. We met each other's friends and started to really develop a connection. But there was one problem I couldn't seem to get over: he was a huge fucking stoner. Personally, I smoked enough pot in high school and wasn't really interested in starting up again. It just isn't my thing. If it were a casual hobby, I'm sure I could get over it, but this was a constant habit.

Every time he smoked, his ego seemed to inflate and I felt like I was there merely as a sounding board for all his grandiose dreams. Acting, he explained, wasn't his end goal. After winning his first Oscar (for either acting or producing, he wasn't quite sure yet) and becoming a Grammy Award–winning recording artist, he planned to become a politician.

"Can politicians smoke pot?" I asked. He ignored the question before showing me his tattoos.

The pot definitely bothered me, but I wasn't ready to end it all just yet. During his next trip to L.A., he invited me to dinner at the swanky restaurant in his hotel. Over dinner, Wade convinced me to smoke with him that night.

"Just one hit," he said, assuring me that it was the perfect night because we wouldn't even leave his hotel room. "I promise, it'll be fun."

I finally relented. #BigFuckingMistake. #JustSayNo.

When we got up to the room, he handed me the pipe and I took a toke, then another, and then one more. Trouble was ahead.

"This isn't like the old stuff," he said. "No hallucinations. No cravings."

For the first few minutes, I was feeling exhilarated and bounced around his massive suite. It was a total out-of-body experience. Then he casually mentioned that he wanted to have a little party in the room, so a few of his friends were coming over. I had already met most of them and was feeling fabulous, so it sounded like a great idea . . . not that I had a say in the matter anyhow.

"Oh, and by the way," he added, "my sister's coming by too."

Fuck me, I thought. He spoke so highly of his family and I had been hearing about his sister for months and months, so of course I would have loved to meet her, but I was high! #Chronic.

A few minutes later, there was a knock on the door. It turns out "a few friends" actually meant about twenty or so people . . . most of whom I'd never met. That's where the pot started to turn on me. This really wasn't like the pot I used to smoke in high school. My paranoia became so intense that I was absolutely positive that everyone in that hotel suite wanted to kill me.

I refused to smoke anything else after that, but there were plenty of fumes in the room that kept me buzzing for the rest of the evening. I desperately wanted to leave but wasn't in any condition to go out into the world, so I holed up in his room by myself and laid in the bed to hallucinate in peace (oh yes, there *were* hallucinations). One by one, people started to leave, and I thought that finally I'd be able to come down from this high and pass the fuck out.

But around one A.M. there was a knock at the door. His sister had finally arrived. I pulled myself together so that he could introduce us. She was beautiful and very light-skinned compared to Wade, which caught me a little off guard. They were both incredibly attractive but couldn't look less alike. Actually, she looked a lot like his "crazy ex-girlfriend" who had confronted me months earlier. Maybe it was the pot, but I started to get skeptical that they were really siblings. I knew his parents were still married, but maybe she was a half sister or something.

That's when shit got strange. After saying hello, she walked over to Wade, who had settled into a chair, and placed herself seductively in his lap. #WTF. I have a brother; I do not sit in his lap *ever*. And if I were forced to, it damn sure wouldn't be sexy. For the next hour, I watched as she flirted with him and caressed him, all the while asking me a million questions about my life, my divorce, and my children.

Are you fucking kidding me? Was this really happening, or was the pot fucking with me that badly? Was he lying to me about who she really is, or was he fucking his sister?

"Okay, honey, I need to ask you a question," I blurted out. "Are you really his sister, or are you a fucking hooker?"

With or without the pot, sometimes I just can't help being Brandi.

A blanket of silence fell over the room. Neither of them said a word.

"It's probably time for you to go to bed," Wade said after what felt like ten minutes.

But she didn't answer my question, I thought.

My word vomit pretty much put an end to the party, and everyone, including his "sister," made an exit. When he finally joined me in the bedroom, he didn't say a word about what had happened and appeared to still be in the mood for some sexy time. I was grateful that he wasn't angry, so even though I wasn't particularly in the mood, and I was on my period, I went with it . . . for the entire hour. When we finished, the white sheets looked like a fucking crime scene. I knew I couldn't stay there. The high had finally worn off, so I got dressed, said good-bye, and did the walk of shame to the hotel taxi line.

We're still friendly and continue to send the occasional naughty text, but we're no longer seeing each other. And thankfully, I learned that the woman who spent the evening seductively perched on my boyfriend's lap wasn't *actually* his sister.

Not all actors are terrible partners. The gay ones pre-tending to be straight for the sake of their film careers and children seem to be devoted husbands capable of maintaining long-lasting relationships with their wives. Sure, they would much rather fuck other men—but at least they're discreet.

Let me be clear. My "just say no" policy also applies to musicians and professional athletes. These types of men feel like they're carrying the weight of the world on their shoulders, which makes them difficult partners. They are constantly surrounded by people paid to fluff their egos. #Fluffers. If you choose to be in a relationship with them, you'll constantly play second fiddle to their career, bank accounts, and all that necessary traveling. You'll need at least three bellhops to assist you with all their fucking baggage. Because at the end of the day, they'll always "come" first—pun intended.

Brandi's

JUST SAY NO TO ACTORS—AND POT.

Tweet-ism

5

Douche Bags,
Part Two

MICRORELATIONSHIP (NOUN)

1. An arrangement between two people that is not significant enough to be considered a legitimate relationship but more meaningful than a casual encounter. 2. The essence of my dating life.

Example: The microrelationship lasted a few months but never went beyond biweekly dinner dates or more than fifteen minutes of oral.

You didn't think I only dated two douche bags while on my journey to find Mr. Right, did you? I've had a handful of microrelationships. I have a theory that most guys are just a *little* douche baggy, but there are degrees of severity, from mildly lame to downright repulsive. Trust me, I was married to one for eight years. I consider myself something of a douche bag expert. When you finally meet a man who you actually want to spend time with despite whatever douche-y flaws he might have, I like to think you've finally met the person you're supposed to be with.

As I spent more time in the dating pool, my sea legs got stronger and I developed a better idea of how to detect the skeeziest of potential suitors—and how to weed them out.

THE NBA PLAYER

He was six feet eleven.

And even wearing my six-inch Christian Louboutin stiletto (I was on crutches at the time), I could still fit perfectly under his arm. We met at the Skybar at the Mondrian hotel (no, I don't actually go there anymore) one summer night and kept locking eyes across the pool. He finally asked if he could buy me a drink. We chatted for a little bit—and it was fun to have to look up to catch his eyes even though I was wearing my one high heel. He was bossy, and I liked it. He told me he was taking me to dinner the next night and asked for my number.

When we arrived at Dan Tana's in West Hollywood

the following evening (Yes, we arrived together. Techni-
cally, wasn't it our second date?), we squeezed into the tiny
booth like two giants in a Volkswagen Bug.

"What should we order?" he asked, looking over the
options.

I didn't need to open my menu; it was practically committed to memory. This was a frequent date-night haunt
for my billionaire ex-boyfriend and me. #DrinkingAnd
Tweeting. Looking back, I think he preferred it for how
big the miniature tables made him feel. I couldn't even
cross my legs (not that I wanted to that night anyway).
Plus, I have four restaurants that I like all within a three-
mile radius of one another: Dan Tana's, Polo Lounge,
Craig's, and E. Baldi.

"I got this," I purred, snatching the menu from him.
The NBA Player smiled and touched the top of my leg.
Our chemistry was electric. He was fair-skinned but stern
looking and rugged—one of those manly men who always
took control, but I would do the ordering tonight. The
sexual tension was thick and had been from the moment
he picked me up in his Porsche Panamera, a "come fuck
me" kind of car. (All the hot guys in L.A. drive either
this . . . or a piece of shit.) The energy between us was out
of control, and even the simplest gestures became sexual.

The waiter came by, and I ordered my staples: extra crispy

fried calamari, all rings (no squigglies); fried mozzarella; the chopped salad; and the veal Milanese with a side of pasta with meat sauce.

Men love women who actually eat. Which brings me to my next piece of advice: ladies, don't think you're doing yourself any favors when you order a small salad with dressing on the side and take four bites before announcing, "I'm so full." It's so much sexier when you have an appetite—and you won't end up devouring a pizza by yourself later that night when you get home.

"He will have the grilled Dover sole," I announced. I could tell he was a healthy eater, and I knew my taking charge of the order would be a total turn-on.

I also knew I couldn't go too overboard in the food department, since I was wearing my new Alexander Wang one-shoulder gray T-shirt dress, which was so tight I couldn't even wear underwear. The dress was a new purchase for the date, and I didn't need a huge pasta belly at the end of the meal. Although the way things were going, I would need to carb up just a bit because it was clear that I would need my energy later. I nibbled on just enough of everything and was perfectly content.

To be honest, I can barely remember what we talked about during dinner. We couldn't keep our hands off each other. Watching one another as we ate became some kind of food foreplay as I dropped a calamari ring on my tongue.

We barely knew each other, but there was such an intense chemistry between us that we powered through dinner so we could quickly get to dessert . . . and I'm not talking about the espresso ice cream.

I didn't even mind (at first) that most of the conversation I *do* remember consisted of him name-dropping his best friend . . . another basketball player who was engaged to an incredibly famous reality star. They were planning a TV wedding that had been the talk of the entertainment world for months. Apparently, there were a lot of perks that came along with having a friend who was marrying into reality TV royalty. I realized then that the NBA Player was not the next great love of my life, but I was pretty sure he was destined to be a pretty great fuck.

By the time I was on my third glass of wine and he was on his third potato vodka, the heat was turning up. His hand found its way under the table and up my dress. (Honestly, with our legs under this incredibly tiny table, it was a wonder that his huge hand could even fit!) I bit my lower lip and stared at him for a second before I started to blush and diverted my eyes. I couldn't wait to feel the scruff on his face, covering his strong jawline, rubbing against my inner thighs. In our minds, we were already fucking. It was on like Donkey Kong.

An hour after we sat down (quick by most standards), he asked if I was ready to go. As we waited at the valet stand, he stood behind me, pressing himself into me while rubbing the sides of my waist. I had to squat down to get into the low car, but luckily there were no paparazzi around to catch my Paris Hilton moment (they'd catch up with me eventually).

His house was approximately five miles from the restaurant, just up Coldwater Canyon in Beverly Hills, but in L.A. it would take about a fifteen-minute drive. I had no idea how we would make it that long.

We didn't.

By the time we hit the canyon road, he was already halfway to fully pleasuring me. We made out like teenagers every time the car hit a traffic light or stop sign. His fingers were all sorts of ways up my dress, and he would look over every few seconds to watch me as I squirmed in the leather seat.

"You have to pull over," I said with heavy breath, my hand making its way over to his lap.

He found a side street and pulled onto it, but we couldn't find a dark spot to park. The streetlights lit up the entire road. When the car was finally in park, I tried to get on top of him, but it was not working in this tiny car. If anyone were actually watching, I'm sure it would have looked hysterical. We were these two huge people trying to sex-wrestle in the front seat of a Porsche.

"This isn't happening," he said. He opened the car door

and we both got out. He easily lifted me up and threw me on the hood of his car, and we went for it. My dress was hiked up around my waist before I could even blink, and he was already inside me. A few seconds later, he flipped me over, and now the front of my body was pressed onto the hood of his car. We were already so turned on that it couldn't have been longer than a few minutes before we were back in the Porsche and headed to his house for round two.

I felt like I was reliving my gymnast days. He flipped me up, tossed me over, and turned me around like I was a doll. I've said it before, but there's really nothing hotter than a man who can make you feel small. And at five feet ten, it's been a rarity for me. He was also shattering my "fancy car, terrible in bed" theory. *Good for him*, I thought.

The sex was pretty fucking amazing, but there were a few casualties of the evening. My new dress was destroyed. Between all the stretching, pulling, and car hooding, it was totally trashed. *Oh well*, I thought. I could always buy a new dress; I couldn't always have sex like that. Apparently, his car was a little worse for the wear as well. He texted me the following day that we put a pretty sizable dent on the hood of his $80,000 Porsche. He let me know it was worth it.

We continued seeing each other for the next few weeks, but I knew it would never develop into anything serious. He started to get a little douche-y, and maybe I'm jaded, but I knew the infidelity stigma associated with professional athletes (especially NBA players). I never wanted to go down that road again. Men who were as sexually ferocious as he was were never going to be monogamous. He proved my point for me when we went out on a group date with some of my girlfriends and a handful of his buddies. The NBA Player spent the entire night flirting with one of my best girlfriends. Strike one.

Perhaps I was too vocal about how amazing the sex was or perhaps his best friend's rising celebrity was getting the better of him, because his messages became increasingly condescending. It is a common epidemic in Hollywood: people think that if they are surrounded by "celebrity," that they too are actually famous. No one cares who you're friends with, dude! Your friend's yacht in the south of France isn't doing shit for me (unless you're invited and can bring a guest, in which case, color me impressed!). In this case, however, it was his friend's fiancée—not even his friend—with all the power. I wanted to say, "That doesn't make you cool. It just makes you part of the entourage." And didn't you watch that show? No one wanted to fuck Turtle. (Although the actor who played him is looking pretty great these days.)

"Want to get lucky tonight?" he texted one afternoon after our group date disaster. Really, dude? You're going to "allow" me to have sex with you? I didn't respond. He sent another text a few hours later that read, "This is your last chance."

Should I be grateful that I get to go down on a guy whose best friend is marrying someone rich and famous? He needed to get the fuck over himself. I wonder if he ever stopped to think that maybe I had something to do with how fucking good the sex was. I happen to know a thing or two.

That was strike two. He was out. (I know it's typically a three-strike rule, but I prefer to play by my own rules.) I stopped responding—the orgasms weren't worth dealing with his inflated ego, and I had moved on to the next guy.

His best friend's "celebrity" marriage lasted for seventy-two whole days—and became the laughingstock of the gossip world. Slowly his friend started to fade from the spotlight, and surprise, surprise, the NBA Player started to reach out to me again. Recently, I ran into him while he was lying out at a hotel pool in West Hollywood. He was there trying to pick up girls. I guess that whole "pseudofamous best friend" thing wasn't working out for him much anymore.

"I'd love to see you," he said a little sheepishly. "You want to grab dinner?"

Oh, how the mighty have fallen, I thought. We haven't slept together since before the reality-wedding debacle, but he still reaches out every few weeks to see if I'm free to grab dinner . . . and then dessert. Maybe he finally realized that he wasn't actually God's gift to women and he should have been a little more concerned with *Keeping Up with Brandi.* I haven't decided whether or not I'll go out with him again. Maybe I will, but first he needs to get an SUV—and some dignity.

THE FALLEN STAR

He was one of the most attractive men I'd ever laid eyes on. Honestly, he looked a lot like my ex-husband—complete with delicious dimples—but he had sparkly aqua-colored eyes, more tousled brown hair, and large chiseled arms covered in tattoos. We first met at a mutual friend's BBQ in Calabasas while I was still married, and I remember thinking he was going to make some lucky girl very happy—and *very* insecure.

Like I said, Valley housewives like to talk, so I quickly learned he was just your typical Hollywood bad boy trying to make a name for himself producing big-budget action movies. After a string of box-office successes, he began getting caught up in L.A.'s party scene and developed some pretty nasty demons. Over the years, I heard stories about his severe drug addiction and was sad to learn he spent most of his time bouncing in and out of rehab facilities. As you can imagine, it pretty much ruined his career. Hollywood loves to celebrate a person on the rise, but the town virtually disappears when he or she begins to fall—which apparently led to one relapse after the other for the Fallen Star. Once again, enter Facebook.

A photo popped up in my news feed of this dark, handsome producer with our mutual friend. It took me a second to register who it was. He looked great—and most importantly, clean. I clicked on his profile and saw many of the AA mantras I've heard over the years, but I didn't notice any kind of strong female presence on the page. #Just Sayin. *The Fallen Star finally got his shit together,* I thought—and, wow, he looked hotter than I remembered. After a glass of liquid courage, I decided to message him and ask if he remembered me (but not before updating my profile picture to my favorite beach bikini photo).

Even though I was married when we first met, I could tell he was definitely interested. Haven't you all learned by now? Just because you're married doesn't necessarily mean you go unnoticed—especially in L.A. Sadly, many guys agree that it's the safest kind of one-night stand imaginable. The married woman's already got someone to cuddle with her, take her to dinner, and provide for her. You know her sexual partners are limited . . . usually. And, most of the time, she's *just* as invested in keeping your little tryst a secret as you are. Unfortunately for him, when we first met I was a one-guy kind of girl.

Either way, I thought a flirty little message couldn't hurt—and if he didn't get back to me, I'd just convince myself that he never checks his Facebook. Right?

I didn't have to worry long, because the Fallen Star responded almost immediately:

"Of course I remember you. How are things?"

We began filling each other in on the past few years. I revealed that I was currently single, and he confided in me his struggles but that he was currently sober. As far as he knew, I had no clue about his drug addiction, so I was impressed that he was so forthcoming. Within hours of my Facebook message, we had plans to see each other when he got back from New York a few days later.

After that first week, we became a daily "thing." Even though we decided to take things slow, we talked every night on the phone for the first week. The Fallen Star seemed sweet, kind, and funny—he also had the sexiest voice of all time. I felt like I was *finally* dating someone "normal." After months and months of dodging bullets left and right, I met someone who liked and respected me the way I deserve.

We did all the boring things couples do that I had been missing: we went to casual dinners at cheesy chain restaurants (#OliveGarden), we saw matinee movies at the mall, and we even went for sunset hikes on warm days. After a couple of weeks of dating, we slept together. The sex wasn't off the hook, but that was okay because it was good . . . and easy. It didn't need to be all *Fifty Shades of Grey* because it felt more like making love. #HopelessRomantic. I really cared about this man. (At this point you're probably wondering what's douche-y about this guy. He doesn't deserve to be in this chapter, but I'm getting to the point.)

One afternoon we were at his high-rise apartment in Santa Monica, which had sweeping views of the ocean. Sure, he was a middle-aged guy with a roommate, but that was probably a good thing considering the Fallen Star was still recovering.

"It must be so peaceful waking up to this every morning," I said.

"It really has been," he said. "Unfortunately, we have to move out."

This caught me totally off guard. Apparently, he and his roommate had been late on the rent for months and were getting evicted from their beachside condo. We were talking every day, and he failed to mention that he would soon be homeless. That didn't seem to me like something that just slips your mind. Nevertheless, he seemed in pretty good spirits. Clearly it was something he wasn't too interested in elaborating on, so I dropped it. He was an adult, so it wasn't my place to pry.

A few days later, he invited me to join him at a friend's birthday party. We arrived at a West Hollywood bar, where I was happy to be this handsome man's arm candy in white skinny jeans, a black silk top, and sky-high heels. After a round of introductions, I excused myself to the ladies' room to check my look in the mirror. When I returned, I was shocked to see the Fallen Star with a beer in his hand. Are you fucking kidding me? I think most people would agree that "sober" has a pretty fucking strict definition.

"What are you doing?" I whispered heatedly, abruptly pulling him away from his conversation.

"It's just a beer," he said, batting those killer aqua eyes at me. I wasn't budging, so he relented: "Look, in these settings it's easier for me to just have a beer or two, maybe smoke a little pot, but that's it. Nothing more."

There were so many things wrong with this, it's not even funny. But he said it so calmly and matter-of-factly, I indulged him for that one evening. I've known a few people close to me who struggle with addiction, and although I had never heard this "just the tip" method with drugs and alcohol, I didn't want to make a scene at this party. Plus, he was getting kicked out of his place. The Fallen Star wasn't showing it, but he had to be under a lot of pressure, right? I knew that he had been scratching and clawing to get back into the moviemaking business, but the rejection of Hollywood was taking its toll on him. Maybe I'd have a talk with him later and encourage him to speak to someone. Either way, I didn't want to seem supportive of these habits, so after the party I told him I wasn't feeling well and wanted to sleep at my house. He seemed surprised but didn't appear to give it too much thought.

I didn't hear from the Fallen Star the following day—or the next, or the next. We had been in constant communication since my Facebook message weeks and weeks earlier, so I was concerned when he went radio silent. I figured he must be upset with me for reprimanding him, so I waited for him to resurface. On the third day, I reached out.

The Fallen Star didn't go home that night after the West Hollywood party. Quite the opposite, actually. He went on a three-day coke-fueled bender with a bunch of his old friends—which included completely destroying a Hollywood hotel room (talk about a cliché!). He hadn't just dipped his toes out of the wagon; he fucking threw himself from it—nose first.

The guilt immediately set in. Was this somehow my fault for not going home with him? Maybe the Fallen Star would have had better luck as an actor than a producer, because apparently his sobriety had been compromised for a while. This was my cue to exit. I didn't want to leave him while at his lowest, but it's common knowledge that people trying to get clean shouldn't be in intimate relationships for the first year of their sobriety. More importantly, I knew he was a good, good man, but he was still on an uphill battle and I wasn't capable of being that kind of support for him. My priorities were my children, and I couldn't split my time.

Not long after, the Fallen Star went back to rehab again. We stayed in touch in the months that followed; I didn't want to totally disappear on him, but I also knew that we could never again be anything more than friends. I wasn't equipped to be anything more than that for him. Recently, I heard from a mutual friend that he had gotten married. It seemed that this latest attempt at sobriety really was working. She even shared a photo with me of the Fallen Star kissing his wife's big, beautiful, pregnant belly. I'm definitely known to be the jealous type, but not this time. It was wonderful to see those sparkly aqua eyes, because I knew he had made it. He was going to be okay.

Brandi's Tweet-ism

KOOL-AID-AHOLICS AND DRUG ADDICTS NEED NOT APPLY.

6

The Booty Call

WALK OF SHAME (NOUN)

The act of leaving an apartment or home (other than your own) the morning after an unplanned sleepover and too much alcohol, wearing the same clothing as the night before, i.e., a cocktail dress.

Example: She wiped the mascara off her face the best she could before quietly sliding back into her tiny bandage dress and doing the walk of shame to the hotel cab line.

I'm pretty sure Shakespeare said it best: "Once a booty call; always a booty call." Or maybe that was just my little gem. Either way, once you become someone's "fuck buddy," it's the point of no return for any other sort of relationship. Let's be honest. Who respects the guy or girl who shows up on your doorstep at eleven P.M. on a weeknight with less than an hour's notice? No one.

If you choose to either employ or become the booty call, here are my suggestions for doing it properly. And yes, there is a "proper" way to have a convenient and purely sexual relationship. I was divorced; I wasn't dead. And even though I am open to loving again, that doesn't mean I don't know how to have a hot one-night stand. No one has *ever* accused me of being a prude.

1. We've all seen *Pretty Woman,* so this one should be pretty obvious: absolutely no kissing! It's far too intimate to be doing with someone who is merely there for sex. Women tend to mistake lust for emotion, so do yourself a favor and compartmentalize. This is not about making love. It's about both of you getting off— otherwise, what's the fucking point? That's not to say you can't enjoy other types of oral pleasure during your booty call, but keep your tongue away from his or her mouth at all costs.

2. Wrap that shit up! Regardless of whether you're the booty caller or the booty callee, it's safe to assume that you are not in a monogamous relationship—you're both probably seeing others or, in my case, seeking the perfect man. So I don't care if you're on the pill or he's had a vasectomy—use a condom! I can't stress this enough. Maybe if my ex-husband had employed this rule, I wouldn't be an HPV statistic.

Yes, I know condoms suck, but I recommend investing in some super-thin ribbed latex ones with flavored lubricant (strawberry's my favorite).

3. Know when to leave. Know when to walk—or rather run—to the door. There is never a reason to sleep over after a booty call. Trust me, people. Maybe you're thinking of the possible morning sex the next day, but do yourself a favor and get the hell out of there. When the sun rises and the booze wears off, your concealer has disappeared, revealing a bright red pimple, and you're suddenly forced into awkward conversation—in the daylight. And no one looks as good in the morning as they did the night before. Is he supposed to suggest breakfast? Or worse, do you enter into the "now what" conversation where you talk about your nonexistent relationship? Hell fucking no. All the other person is probably thinking is: Walk to my front door and see yourself out! Let it be noted that your sexy little

outfit seems more appropriate exiting under the dark of night versus at ten o'clock the next morning when you have mascara smeared across your eyes. Talk about a walk of shame.

4. Choose your booty calls wisely. If it's someone you've had an emotional relationship with recently or have newly broken up with, having sex again is a terrible idea. All it does is stir up old shit that you're both trying to move the hell on from. I suggest calling someone or accepting the invitation of someone you've had a casual, no-strings-attached relationship with in the past or who has already been placed neatly in your friend box (see chapter 7).

5. Booty calls are like tennis. You want to be the one serving. You want control of the ball in your court. And when you say "love," it should only be in reference to the scoreboard.

I'd like to spend just another moment revisiting number four. Now, I'm not trying to get preachy, but I don't understand the need for the hookup apps. Can anyone explain to me why this is a good idea? Grinder has been around for the gay community for quite some time, but

Tinder has recently exploded (pun intended) around the straight world. I know that guys are somehow more capable of having nonemotional sex, but most women have a pretty difficult time cutting off the heartstrings. If you choose to engage in a one-night stand, shouldn't you do it with someone you trust or have been with before? These apps are like a virtual meat market for men to pick and choose. Wake up, ladies. It's 2014. Don't you have any self-respect? If you're looking for love, go to a bar in a provocative little black dress like a normal woman. If you're looking to get laid, call someone you know!

As for the guys, most of the men I know are currently using the app just on the off chance that they have some free time during the day and need to find the closest, hottest girl who's down for a quick, no-strings-attached bang.

It really is a whole new level of grossness.

Are you guys so fucking lazy that you need an app to help you choose between a collection of "casual" women within your current three-mile radius to screw? I just don't get it. Half the fun of sex—and dating, for that matter—is the chase and the challenge. So I don't see the fun in a wham-bam-thank-you-ma'am. I'd rather stick with a drawer full of kitty toys and ask one of my guy friends to take me to dinner.

Truth be told, I'm no longer interested in just booty calls. Spending a few hours banging someone who I see no future with is taking me off the market. Maybe I'm maturing or evolving, but casual sex isn't that appealing to me anymore. The new Brandi wants to focus on staying open to having a committed and long-lasting relationship. I'm ready to forever forgo the concept of the booty call. #New Woman.

But ask me about it again tomorrow.

Brandi's

VIBRATORS MAKE GREAT ONE-NIGHT STANDS.

Tweet-ism

7

The Friend Box

FRIEND BOX (NOUN)

1. The mental compartment where you place someone you have no interest in pursuing romantically but would like to keep in your life for friendship and other perks.

2. A place with high walls, strict rules, and a no reentry policy. #PunIntended.

Example: While the celebrity chef was mediocre in the bedroom, he was a wizard in the kitchen, and so I decided to place him in my friend box.

My journey toward "happily ever after" was not going as well as I had hoped—and there were only so many days I could casually hang around the Beverly Hills Whole

Foods looking for single, attractive men. Were there options I wasn't already exploring? Besides leaving the city entirely, I wasn't sure what else to do to ramp up my search.

A close girlfriend pointed out the fact that I already had a wonderful group of men in my life and suggested that maybe I was overlooking some of the prospects in my own backyard.

Let's not fool ourselves; men and women can very rarely be friends without at least one party imagining what it would be like to fuck the other—or at least have one awkward drunken moment at a pool party where there's a bit of wishful thinking. . . . It's completely normal. #Right? When you get along so well, you can't help but consider the what-ifs. And like many other women before me, I too had dabbled in my friend box.

MY OTHER EX-HUSBAND

I married my best friend New Year's Day in Las Vegas. I was proving a point, so it sounded like a really great idea at the time. Like I always say, I am known for offering the best relationship advice. #DoAsISayNotAsIDo.

Honestly, it was a joke. We didn't get a marriage license and never planned to; we were just being single and silly. Darin had joined my three girlfriends and me in Vegas for the holiday. During a boozy dinner at Nobu inside the

Hard Rock Hotel, we joked about all the different insane things we could do to ring in 2012—my first New Year's Eve as an officially single lady (translation: divorce finalized!). Skydiving? Fuck no. I have trouble even getting *on* an airplane; you will never catch me jumping out of one. Tattoo? Never! This MILF doesn't do body ink. Steal Mike Tyson's tiger? Already been done.

"How hilarious would it be if we got married?" Darin suggested. Everyone laughed, but the conversation continued snowballing.

"You never follow through with shit, Darin," I said. That put an end to the conversation for the night, and I rang in the new year as a single lady and kissed my girlfriends as the clock struck midnight.

The next day, we were nursing our mutual hangovers and decided to catch a showing of the newest *Mission: Impossible*. I was popping Junior Mints in my mouth, chilling in my comfy workout clothes, and waiting for the previews to start when Darin brought it up again.

"We should totally get married," he said, smirking.

"Okay," I deadpanned, looking straight at him.

Two hours later, we were pulling up in a cab outside the Wedding Chapel on Las Vegas Boulevard, and I married my best friend in black stretch pants, a white long-sleeved Izod shirt, no makeup, and a pair of Puma tennis shoes. I never could have imagined what a big deal it would become. At the time, I was still navigating the world of so-cial media and was still relatively new to the public eye, so I thought it was a hilarious idea to tweet out a picture of our "wedding" to all my "tweeples." Honestly, who spends their wedding night in the VIP room of the Spearmint Rhino strip club? The next morning, we woke up in our "marital" bed—still fully dressed, mind you—to hundreds of texts, e-mails, and phone calls. Our fake wedding had become one of 2012's first big news stories. My friends told me that it was the number one trending story on the Internet. (I still don't know what the fuck that means, but apparently it was a big deal.) We immediately started damage control, but I can tell you this, even with all the media attention, my sec-ond divorce was much easier than my first.

Moral of the story: what happens in Vegas doesn't al-ways stay in Vegas. #BrandiBlunder. Social media ruined that for everyone. Las Vegas needs to get a new slogan. (Side note: While I've always respected the institution of marriage, I realize now that it was an insensitive thing to do, as many of the people I love most in my life were, at the time, still fighting for their right to be married.)

Darin and I have a complicated relationship. He's been one of the few men in my life who I've been able to count on for better or worse, through sickness and health, and I know it will be only death that could tear us apart. We didn't need to sign any papers or have a fancy party to commit our lives to one another. We just did. He's even better than a real husband, because he doesn't have to be there. He wants and chooses to be there.

He's my best friend—and nothing more (like 95 percent of the time). Our close friends often encourage us to be together romantically, saying that we're perfect for each other. They're right. We are perfect for each other, but there are a few pretty big roadblocks on our journey to "happily ever after": we fight like brother and sister, we have zero sexual attraction, and I think I remind him a little too much of his ex-wife. While I've heard many sad, sad stories about sexless marriages, I never intend to be in one.

Let me backtrack just a bit for you. Darin went through his divorce a few years before my ex-husband and I. His divorce was contentious and dirty, so both he and his ex-wife knew what I was up against. Darin and I initially met through his ex-wife, who had been a close friend of mine. She stood by my side during the height of the tabloid scandal—which meant neighboring lounge chairs at a posh Beverly Hills hotel, all courtesy of my ex-husband's credit card. It was hardly a rough gig. But when I found myself going down a destructive path with her, I realized I needed to purge the negative influences in my life. You can interpret that however you like.

That's when Darin reentered my life. He and his ex-wife were on friendly terms at the time (and continue to be) and share custody of their son, who just so happens to be Mason's best friend. Those two lovable knuckleheads are joined at the hip, and since his ex-wife and I no longer could coordinate play dates, Darin and I started spending time together again. We quickly came to rely on each other when it came to the kids, and it was a huge relief.

Regardless of what means you have at your disposal (and Darin has a lot, ladies!), being a single parent is tough. It's been great having him help with last-minute soccer practice, pick up a sick kid at school, or even take me and the kids to dinner when my license was suspended (no, not for the DUI; I hadn't mailed in my registration on time, and I was not going to risk driving and get into any more run-ins with the Beverly Hills Police Department). And on the flip side, when Darin had a last-minute hot date or needed to head to Vegas with a client, my home was always open to his son for a sleepover. I was happy to oblige. In a strange way, since we haven't had much luck coparenting with our ex-spouses, we rely on each other to help. He also fills the "dude" role in my life. When my beloved dog of twelve years Jesse was attacked by coyotes in my backyard (something that still breaks my heart every day and made the loss of Chica so much worse), it was Darin who came over to take care of the situation because I was inconsolable and physically unable to handle it myself. If my electricity shut down in the middle of the night, it was Darin who came over to fix it. Sure, he would complain a little and joke that I owe him a blow job, but don't all fake husbands? As a single mom, we all need a man sometimes—after all, who else are you going to call when you need help hanging your new flat-screen television? (I used to call him to help me kill spiders, but after a few years of living in the hills I've learned how to take them out myself! #Progress!)

He's a catch. I've always known this and have even tried setting him up with every one of my single girl-friends. I'd be lying if I said we never slept together. It happened once after a Memorial Day BBQ and never again. I'm a lot of things, but a liar is not one of them. Sure, it got weird for a day or two, but we managed to move forward. We love each other. In many ways, he's my soul mate, but we're just not meant to share our lives together in a romantic way. Plus, when it comes to the sex stuff, we just don't click. I've always been the most attracted to ass-holes, and Darin just isn't one. #BrandiProblems.

But most importantly, the risk of it not working out and having to remove him from my life would be like divorce all over again and is simply not worth it—to either of us. When he does finally meet the perfect woman for him, I hope she can understand and appreciate our friendship. When I find my partner, he'll have to deal with it too.

So while we married in Las Vegas and it was never really legal, my second husband will always be my favorite husband. And I don't need a piece of paper to know that he'll always be loyal to me.

THE BOY WONDER

He was like a real-life version of "Eloise at the Plaza."

At twenty-eight years old, Asher was an accomplished filmmaker who resided in one of the most exclusive and luxurious hotels in Los Angeles. Yes, he actually lived in a hotel. He was a rare breed of native-born Angeleno who was raised alongside the rich and powerful of Beverly Hills—his classmates were the sons and daughters of billionaires, Oscar-winning actors, and media moguls. Growing up, Asher was waited on hand and foot, so when it came time to move out, the idea of fending for himself— albeit in a multimillion-dollar apartment in L.A.'s prestigious Wilshire Corridor with a full-time staff—was still a little unsettling. Instead, he decided to move into a hotel where life would be just a bit more civilized. This didn't seem like a huge stretch, since he spent many years as a child living at the Beverly Hills Hotel. For Asher, this was a normal kind of lifestyle.

Each morning, his signature breakfast was just a phone call and fifteen minutes away. Upon its arrival, the staff would use the opportunity to whisk away Asher's laundry from the day before in order to return it each night fluffed and folded during turndown service. As soon as he exited the property for the day, the housekeeping staff would buzz about his suite, restocking fluffy white towels, organizing his bathroom, making the bed, and freshening up the floral arrangements.

All of that aside, he was an exceptionally down-to-earth guy—relatively speaking. Despite the success he had already found, Asher was still a little boy in so many ways. He'd arrive for dinner in a Polo shirt with the oversized Ralph Lauren brand logo, jeans, sneakers, and a mop of messy brown hair on top of his head. He could make conversation with just about anyone and, most importantly, had a heart of gold. I credit that to a fantastic upbringing. Sure, he was spoiled rotten, but he had two loving parents and a really close-knit family.

We were introduced when a mutual friend tried to set us up on a blind date. Apparently, Asher had a "thing for cougars." After a few weeks of texting back and forth, the conversation began to fizzle. I wasn't too eager to attempt another blind date—even though I could google him if I wanted to, I was never interested enough to do the work. And, truth be told, he wasn't too aggressive in pursuing me either. I chalked it up to timing and didn't think twice about it.

It wasn't until months later that I *actually* met him at the Polo Lounge (my home away from home).

"I know you," I joked. "We were supposed to go on a date, and then you went MIA." He apologized profusely and explained to me that his dog had passed away. Apparently he took it pretty hard, as anyone would, so he had a difficult few months. That's Asher for you: a sensitive little rich boy with a bleeding heart.

Regardless of the awkward introduction, we hit it off immediately. We spent hours that night just getting to know each other, but there was nothing romantic about it. It felt like I was having an evening on the town with an old friend. I joked that we were like the Golden Girls (I was Blanche, and he was Dorothy), which was a red flag that anything intimate would never really work. If I didn't want to fuck him from the moment I met him (and I didn't), I would never develop the kind of passion I was looking for in a partner.

Hollywood loves to make those romantic comedies about two friends who live side by side for years only to discover, after years of heartbreak and disappointment with other partners, that they were soul mates all along.

It just doesn't work like that in real life. Sure, you could grow to want to fuck someone over time, but if that fire isn't there from square one, it will eventually fizzle again. Asher was dependable, successful, kind, and generous—all the things that were great on paper—but we had zero sexual chemistry. He was still in his twenties—there's no way a man in his twenties could fuck me the way I needed it. Plus, his best friend played a dorky, suspender-sporting geek on a popular nineties television show. Literally. How could I ever take a guy seriously who wanted to double-date with that guy?

Even though I still considered him a kid, I came to rely on him for advice and guidance, although I do blame him for missing that "epic" Brendan Fraser party (see chapter 3). On that particular evening, I actually went back to Asher's hotel room and slept next to him in bed, but he never made a move.

Therefore, I immediately concluded that he must be gay. That sounds pretty egotistical, but that's not how I mean it. When you take a girl back to your hotel room after a night of drinking, it's almost obligatory that you at least *try* to make a move—as long as she's reasonably lucid. At two A.M. in the dark, everyone sort of looks the same and sex is fun, but he didn't touch a hair on my head.

It wasn't until after my dog Chica went missing more than a year after we met that we finally slept together. He had offered to stay with me for a few days after it happened, because supposedly someone had broken into my house and I was terrified to stay there alone until my new, high-tech security system was installed. We spent the evening drinking and gossiping like old women do (#GoldenGirls,

#ImStillBlanche)—until something changed in his eyes. He was hungry for me.

Under normal circumstances, I would have refused his advances. His friendship had become so important to me that I didn't want anything to jeopardize that, but I was so emotional after losing my puppy that I was in a highly vulnerable and semi-intoxicated state. I knew that spending an hour fooling around might take my mind off of what had happened, so I went with it.

For the sake of our friendship, I'm going to opt for a rare moment of discretion when talking about sex with Asher. I actually couldn't tell you much about it if I wanted to. I barely remember it, except for the fact that he never even took off his shirt.

The next morning, I thought it would be funny to tell him that I had thought he was gay.

"Why would you think that?" he asked.

"That night after the art show with the felon, I slept in your bed topless, and you didn't make a move," I explained, pouring myself a cup of coffee. It was unusually normal between us the next morning—like he immediately went back to being my best friend.

"That's because I was disgusted by you," he said nonchalantly. "You were sitting in the back of the car on a date with a coked-up criminal."

After he burst my bubble, I realized he made a valid point.

We started casually dating—and it was nice. Despite being more than ten years younger than me, he treated me how a grown-ass man should treat a woman, and it was easy to fall under his spell. He sent town cars to pick me up for our dates, he always picked up the check at dinner, and he had fresh flowers sent to my house every few days. He even offered the services of his assistant when I was booking travel or in need of an extra pair of hands. #LAProblems.

But I knew our relationship was destined for failure. Besides the fact that I needed to get drunk to actually have sex with him (#BadFuckingSign), the kid would constantly flirt with my girlfriends. Come on, dude. That's like the first rule of being a good boyfriend. He would sit next to me, rub my leg, and make subtly veiled sexual references to other women—and not just any women, my fucking friends. I know a lot of people say they're just "natural flirts," but when you have a relationship history as colored as mine, you become a little more sensitive to that kind of shit. And seriously, he just needed to learn how it works. I actually have a theory that the biggest cheats are the guys who *won't* take their eyes off of you all night, but as soon as you're out of sight, they have a pussy posse at their beck and call.

When it came to game play, Asher was still pitching in the minors. I needed a seasoned major league veteran, like the boyfriend equivalent of Derek Jeter. (Wait, is Derek Jeter single? Maybe I should just date him.) After a few weeks of dating, I told Asher that we should just keep things platonic. He's too important to me to ever risk losing him, but he's not mature enough to know how to fuck me. However, he does know how to make me laugh—and that's a really good thing.

Almost every guy I've placed in the friend box has at one point or another tried to get inside my *real* box. If you're both single and enjoy spending time together, why wouldn't you think about the possibility of being together? So you do what every normal, red-blooded American should do: you don't officially date, but you make him or her your fallback plan on Saturday nights because friends, even ones who eventually sleep together, don't have to break up when it doesn't work out. After you realize the romantic aspect of the relationship isn't working for one reason or the other, this doesn't mean you should just toss him aside!

On the contrary, you just need to compartmentalize him. Every woman needs a handful of men to keep in the friend box. I mean maybe they're good with computers or they offer to watch your dogs or they have floor tickets to the Lakers or they hang out with cool people like Dr. Dre—all of these are acceptable reasons to keep men around. However, it's time to "friend"-label them—or place them back in the *appropriate* box. Sex just confuses things, and I already have trouble with that. #DontGetIt Twisted. #GetItStraight.

Here I offer my guide on when to "friend" your man.

1. When he flirts with your friends. This one is a no-brainer. If he's brazen enough to flirt with other people right in front of you, what is he capable of when your back is turned?

2. When you require at least three drinks to sleep with him and he only wants to have sex in the bed. #FriendBoxNotMyBox.

3. When you care if he has bad breath. Sure, you never want to make out with someone who tastes like garlic or tobacco, but would you stop in the middle to tell him to hit up the Scope because you're so grossed out that he's breathing all over your $400 Jennifer Adams sheet set? Or are you so into the moment that you just couldn't care less? If it's the former, it's time to put him in the friend box.

4. When he is more concerned with other people's opinions than yours.

5. If he is more than ten years younger than you, do yourself a favor and stop now. It's never going to work. You might be the hot older woman now, but what happens in ten or twenty years? What happens when he's at his physical and sexual peak and you're on the slow descent? Let Demi Moore learn that lesson for all of us.

Brandi's

JUST BECAUSE YOU DON'T WANT TO FUCK HIM, DOESN'T MEAN YOU DON'T WANT TO USE HIS JONATHAN BEACH CLUB MEMBERSHIP.

Tweet-ism

8

Dating and
Parenting

COPARENTING (NOUN . . . MYTH)

1. The act of two individuals sharing legal and physical custody of a child or children.

2. When two grown-ass people attempt to put personal differences aside so they can do what's best for the children they share.

Example: Although coparenting, both were still acting like children themselves. #Immature.

Mason and Jake aren't allowed to bring their "nice" clothes to Mom's house.

That basically sums up our coparenting or, as I call it, "no-parenting." The boys have every video game imaginable (not to mention the iPods, iPads, iRobots, and M-Macs), while I still struggle with my fucking BlackBerry. They have a closet full of designer clothes at Dad's Hidden Hills estate in Calabasas. (My ex-husband keeps his new wife deep in The Valley too.) Sadly, when it's time to come to my house, they are forced to change into the exact same clothes I sent them over to Dad's house in two days earlier. Apparently, they each have a "Brandi" pile in their room—not even a "Mom"pile—of the things they are allowed to bring with them for their time at my house. It's like my ex-husband's worried I'll ruin Mason's laptop computer on purpose or "accidentally" throw out the outrageously expensive jeans they bought Jake.

I didn't even flinch (okay, maybe a little) when I heard news that my ex-husband was *finally* able to move into his dream home in Hidden Hills. Good for him. He deserves it. Right? According to the boys, the house has a giant pool, a tree house, a zip line, a tricked-out movie theater, a custom trampoline, and—wait for it—a rock-climbing wall. I mean, how can you expect children to ever be happy without a ridiculous structure they use ten times before getting bored? Essentially, they have a fucking theme park in their backyard. I can't compete with that, and I gave up trying long ago. Still, it isn't easy.

My ex-husband and I continue to discuss the well-being of our children via our assistants. (Full disclosure:

my assistant only works part-time and only while I'm filming. #CheaperThanANanny.) I have a phone number for their house now, although it's a line that never actually works. However, I'm still blocked from calling his cell phone. My ex-husband had a yearlong affair with this woman (and many, many others) through his cell phone, so I guess I can understand her paranoia. Funnily enough, I'm the last woman she ever has to worry about sleeping with her husband. #HadItFirst. Despite what the gossip websites report about heated run-ins and "Twitter wars," things have gotten a lot better between us. Yes, my ex-husband's new wife sent me a bouquet of beautiful flowers on Mother's Day—it was a nice gesture, but about four years too late. #Progress. Their father and I mainly communicate via e-mail. (Although I rarely get a reply unless I copy my assistant on it. He wouldn't want anyone else to know what a narcissistic asshole he is, plus my assistants are cute young girls and he's a flirt. #JustSayin.) It's the best way to keep our conversations civil and focused on our boys, because every phone conversation ends up getting so heated that one of us hangs up on the other and nothing gets resolved. Especially when he's not working. #JustSayNoToActors.

Unfortunately, he still doesn't consult me when making larger decisions about the boys that two parents *should* discuss. For example, I wasn't asked my opinion when he decided to take our ten-year-old son to see an R-rated movie. He's still a baby in so many ways, and I don't think it's appropriate. Call me old-fashioned. (Seriously. I rarely get to be called that.) Needless to say, I wasn't thrilled when both of my sons were given BB gun assault rifles for Christmas. I may sound like the mother in *A Christmas Story*, but for real, they'll shoot their eyes out! They're ten and six. Guns, of any kind, are not an appropriate gift for little boys—or for any of us, for that matter. Don't even get me started on their fully operational motorized dirt bikes intended for grown-ass people. I'm a nervous Nellie when it comes to my children. Couldn't he just teach them how to play basketball or tennis? Something that requires a little one-on-one time? News flash: kids crave the actual attention of their parents. My boys are all I have, and I want to shield them and protect them for as long as I can. Also, don't you think giving their mother a heads-up on such important purchases is in order? The truth is, I have no control over what my ex-husband chooses to do during his time with our children. That's not to say I don't get royally pissed off, but all I can do is scream into a pillow and take deep breaths. The boys love their fancy toys—what little kids wouldn't—and as I said in my first book, I had to stop competing. I couldn't keep up with the lavish life they led half the week. I had come to depend on these boys as the men in my life—and I don't like sharing. Over in Calabasas, they have a big house and expensive toys, but what hurts the most is that they have a complete family.

In my heart, I know that Mason and Jake have everything they could ever want when they're with me. But I can't help but wonder, do they still feel my home is somehow incomplete? #CarrieBradshawInspired.

"You don't need a boyfriend," Mason told me. He was just six years old when his father and I decided to separate amid a tabloid-fueled affair, but Mason was ready to assume the role as "the man" in my life. For a while, he did fill those shoes and the empty space next to me on my mattress. This little man offered me the kind of unconditional love that I needed in order to heal. As fucked up as it may sound, I felt safe with my little boys—safer than I would with any grown-ass cheating man. For that, I'm forever grateful to them both.

Like all children, my boys are growing up. At ten years old, Mason is now a full-fledged tween. Holding mom's hand at the grocery store is no longer socially acceptable. And saying, "I love you" in front of his friends? Forget it. Instead, Mason and I developed a secret handshake involving three firm squeezes, to relay the message to one another in public. But behind closed doors, I can always depend on my firstborn to cuddle up next to me during a movie and ask me to write on his back before bedtime. I'm not trying to damage his street cred by any means, but he's the best sort of sensitive I've ever met.

Jake is now six years old, the same age Mason was during the split, but he's a little more gangster. He tests me regularly before flashing me the brightest smile you can imagine, with dimples that would make Mario Lopez jealous.

"Jakey," I told him one summer afternoon. "Just because you smile at me doesn't make smearing marshmallow goo all over my table okay."

"It works with everyone else," he responded with a shrug and went back to his Lego fortress. I couldn't help but laugh out loud, which of course prompted my little troublemaker to look up and flash me yet another big smile to show off those adorable dimples.

Watch out, ladies. He's going to be a heartbreaker. You heard it here first.

Despite their differences as kids, they both agree on one thing: It's now time for Mommy to get a boyfriend. Jake is all of a sudden requesting a "bonus dad," and while the term makes my skin crawl, I can't help but appreciate the sentiment. Nowadays, any man who comes to our front door—the UPS guy, the landscaper, or the electrician— they see as a potential suitor for me. When one of my gay friends or friends' husbands comes to the house, Mason and Jake are all over him like white on rice.

"Can you throw me in the pool?" is one of Jake's first and favorite questions. They're boys—they want to wrestle, throw a football, and play video games. I try to fill that role as much as I can, but they're hungry for masculine attention. And it breaks my heart that this is the one thing I can't give them.

"Mom, I think it's time for you to get married again," Mason recently announced. WTF? When did this change in him happen?

One afternoon, the boys and I were shopping at our neighborhood grocery store, Gelson's. (Yes, I know it's overly expensive, but it's close to my house and sometimes convenience overshadows price. I make up for it with frequent 99 Cent Store and Walmart visits.) We were standing in line at the register when a very cute, very tan, very young guy asked me if I surfed. I may look like a beach bunny in paparazzi pictures, but I am *not* a surfer girl.

"I'd be happy to give your kids some free surf lessons," he offered. He was covered in tattoos and was wearing one of those trucker hats tilted to the side. He couldn't have been more than twenty years old.

Immediately, I saw their eyes light up. Of course they wanted to surf with this seemingly super-cool young guy.

He looked like the sort of dude you'd see on TV during those extreme BMX competitions.

"That's so nice of you, but no thank you," I said. "I really don't want my kids to get eaten by sharks." No one's ever accused me of being rational. He smiled at me, flashing the kind of pearly whites you see in a gum commercial, and walked out of the store. After we checked out, the surfer boy ran up to me in the parking lot and handed me his phone number scribbled on the back of a receipt.

"Thanks," I said through a laugh. His persistence made me smile.

After we loaded the trunk, Mason looked at me and said, "Mom, he seems like a good guy. Why don't you marry him?"

That's when I realized two very important things: (1) I would need to have a conversation with Mason about what constitutes a relationship. If he runs off proposing to his first girlfriend, I'm screwed. (2) It was time to turn up the heat on my search for Mr. Right—and no longer Mr. Right Now. It was a decision I had already made, but I'd been dragging my feet, largely because of Mason and Jake. If I began seriously dating again, I would run the risk of finding someone I would fall in love with . . . and might one day have to introduce to my kids. Making another person a part of my children's world is a really big fucking decision— and I'm not the type of person who takes that lightly.

During the height of my divorce, Mason would get so mad when a man looked at me sideways. He used to say, "We have a daddy. We don't need another one," but now, he's trying to *give* me away to a guy I exchanged ten words with at the grocery store! Talk about a 180! I guess it no longer mattered if I was ready . . . because they were.

In their young eyes, Mommy getting married equals Jake and Mason getting a new live-in playmate.

"Mason, what do you think it means if Mommy gets married again?" I asked him. Even though I don't foresee myself getting married again, I wasn't prepared to explain the concept of "domestic partnership" to my ten-year-old son.

"I don't know," he said, barely looking up from his handheld Nintendo DS. I asked him to put the video game down and answer me again. He thought about it for a moment before saying, "It means that you have someone to hang out with when we're at Dad's and someone to go on vacation with. I don't want you to ever be lonely."

Tears filled my eyes. It was the simple definition of a child, sure, but it was pretty fucking spot on. #SmartBoys. I *did* want someone to spend my days with when I was missing my boys like crazy. While my boys are now used to fancy vacations every few weeks, he was right, traveling was such an important part of my life before I met my ex-husband and I'd like to spend more time showing my family the world.

"I think it means we'll have someone to take us to Disneyland and no one will have to sit alone on the rides!" Jake shouted.

"I'm sure if I got married we'd go to Disneyland once in a while, but not every day," I explained. "Being married means having that person with us all of the time. It means that Mommy will have another person she needs to spend time with too. You guys will have to share me."

I paused, waiting to see how they would react to this. When my boys are with me, they get 100 percent of my attention. Sharing the spotlight with a new guy might not be the easiest transition for them. But the boys were quickly losing interest in the conversation, so I decided this would be a good place to end it for now. We could take up the concept of Mommy "kissing" someone new at a later time or perhaps when I actually met someone special. #BabySteps.

I'll admit, it is hard being just three sometimes. It's a hard number. It's always two against one whenever we play board games. And at dinner, one of us is always sitting alone on the other side of the booth. Instead of playing with my boys, I end up refereeing. I long for the days when we were four—not because I miss my marriage, but because it was easier—and look forward to the days when we will be an even number again.

Mason and Jake have very privileged little lives in so many ways. They have a mom and dad who love them to the moon and back, and they always have food in their bellies and fun getaways on their calendar and not to mention enough toys to fill a Dumpster! But it hasn't been a normal upbringing (although, neither was mine). Photographers follow them in cars whenever they leave the house—whether they're with Mommy or Daddy. They're on airplanes more often than most businessmen and have spent countless nights sleeping on bunk beds driving across the country in a tour bus. You know what? They love every minute of it. Despite the opulence in their world, I hope to instill in them practical life lessons: always say "please" and "thank you," treat others the way you want to be treated, there's no substitute for hard work, and every decision you make has consequences. They're happy, well-rounded boys who managed to come out of a terrible divorce relatively unscathed and not needing therapy. I must give their dad and me kudos for that.

I like to think that, in their eyes, I handled myself properly and made them proud. Of course I'm aware that one day they'll read these books and be able to google every detail of what happened between their father, their "bonus mom," and myself, but for now they're protected from all of that. They'll never be able to remember me speaking ill of their father or his new wife, because I never have (at least not in front of them, which given the circumstances is a huge fucking accomplishment). I'm doing my very best to shape them into good little men with a conscience and manners—despite the occasional potty word (but, come on, all kids do it!). I mean, even I got it from somewhere. #ThanksDad.

It's hard enough dating at forty years old. It's even harder once you're branded as a scorned "divorcée"—because that immediately implies you're carrying around some heavy baggage. It might be the entire Louis Vuitton travel collection, but it's still fucking baggage. If you're me, you also have a trail of paparazzi and a "reality star" label. But once you add children to the mix, it's an entirely different beast.

To this day, I still haven't introduced any man to my children as "my boyfriend." In fact, only a select few have ever gotten the privilege of meeting them at all—and always under a different label. When I do decide to introduce them to someone as my partner, it'll be someone who I'm certain will be around for the long haul.

When I started dating the Surfer, he took an immediate interest in meeting my children. (Not the grocery store surfer, another surfer, a professional one.) Most guys freak out at the idea—fearing any additional responsibilities that might come along with such an important introduction. Not this surfer. He was a chill, "hang ten," salt-of-the-earth kind of guy. We dated for a few months before I finally considered it.

"It can only be as my friend," I told him. He understood. He always understood. He was a good man, with a good heart and an even better body (which allowed me to overlook his annoying fucking dog).

He was a forty-five-year-old professional surfer-turned-artist who lived with his grandmother in Pacific Palisades. To be fair, he claimed he only stayed at her home to help take care of her and the property. (If he's forty-five, his grandmother must have been ancient.) It almost felt like his own place . . . almost. He had the entire bottom floor to himself, which included a bedroom, a hot plate, and a freezer that created a pool of condensation on the floor, but he had an amazing view of the Pacific Ocean. Plus, he was an artist, which meant he was amazing with his hands (in more ways than one). There is some unspoken rule about creative types that allows them to get away with shit that normal nine-to-fivers can't. I was all in. It didn't hurt it was a multimillion-dollar estate just blocks from the water, and he was a struggling artist who spent most of his days at the beach. His tanned skin was weathered from years in the sun and salt water. He was so handsome and had a killer body kept sculpted by daily surf sessions.

When I finally agreed to let him meet Mason and Jake, I thought for a long time about what I would tell them. The Surfer was the first man I'd be introducing them to who I was in a relationship with, and it made me nervous. Sure, they'd been around my guy friends before—but most of them were gay. I want to raise my children to be very open-minded and accepting of all people, so we've had very open conversations about what it means to be gay and straight in this world. It's not a decision; it's just who you were born to be. That's it.

That's when it dawned on me. I'll just tell them he's gay—and remind them that it's not polite to point out this fact or to ask him any personal questions. (I also have to remind them not to say the words "divorced" or "old" to Mom. Little kids have a way of picking up on your sensitivities.)

The Surfer suggested we all go to dinner and bowling.

"Boys, we're going to meet Mommy's friend tonight," I said.

"Is he your *boy*friend?" Jake asked, with a devilish grin on his face. I hadn't really discussed dating around my children, but that doesn't mean they don't quiz me about it all the time. Jake likes to ruffle my feathers, while Mason is genuinely concerned about me spending time alone.

"Of course, he's not my boyfriend," I responded, tickling his stomach. "Actually, he's gay." I regretted saying it as soon as it fell from my lips. Like most things, it sounded a lot better in my head. It was clear I had a fear of recommitting even then.

It's not that I was embarrassed about the Surfer—he was beautiful and wonderful—but I knew he wouldn't be around forever. Sure, he liked to open car doors and hold my hand in the movie theater, but it just wasn't love—and at that age, he should really have his own place, let alone be able to afford to go to a fancy dinner once in a while.

We met the Surfer at Islands restaurant in Calabasas for an early dinner. Jake immediately took to him. I could have bottled the testosterone at the table. The boys began calling him "the Silver Surfer" because of the grayish silvery strips mixed in with his long, sandy brown hair. Jake loves the ocean and stared at him in awe when the Surfer told them a story about a school of dolphins that swam alongside him while he surfed earlier that week.

By the time we got to the bowling alley, Jake had found his new best friend. Mason was impressed too, but at ten years old, he's under a lot of pressure to "play it cool."

"I'm on the Silver Surfer's team," Jake announced when we were tying up our bowling shoes. There was something about that moment that warmed my heart. We were complete, we were (big sigh) . . . four. Mason and I would take on Jake and the Silver Surfer. Everyone had a teammate.

We spent that night laughing, teasing one another, and doing goofy bowling strike victory dances.

There was a reason my children liked him so much: he was a sixteen-year-old boy trapped in a forty-five-year-old man's body. I wasn't looking for a third child; I was looking for someone to actually take care of me on occasion. I had already stayed in one relationship longer than I should have for my children, so I couldn't do that again.

I started to slow things down with him before finally ending things all together. I wanted to leave things on friendly terms, so that maybe we could still go bowling once in a while with Mommy's "gay surfer friend."

Like I said, I haven't yet met the lucky man who will be introduced to my children as Mom's boyfriend. And I'm not quite sure when—or who—that will be. Like with most things, I never think there's a perfect time, but I do feel that certain stars need to align. Here are the rules I've set for myself:

1. The Boyfriend and I need to be in an exclusive, committed relationship for more than six months. That means his Tuesday night poker games aren't actually code for banging a cocktail waitress.

2. He must introduce the idea of meeting my children. I want him to have a genuine interest in meeting the two most important men in my life—and not the other way around. I'm a package deal, and my partner will need to accept that.

3. We need to have an open conversation about what it means for him to meet my kids. When guys hear buzzwords like "commitment," "responsibility," and "long-term," it usually sends them into a spiral. (This is why I never say them. I will use code words like "mature" and "down the road" to trick them so I don't send them running toward the door.) Before the meeting, I will need to test the waters. I have to feel confident that he will be a part of their lives for at least the foreseeable future. If he's incapable of having a simple conversation about what that responsibility means even in non-girlfriend code, how would he actually be able to pull it off if given the chance?

4. The Boyfriend needs to introduce me to *his* family first, and it has to be his idea. I realize this sounds like a double standard, but unless he has young children, I think it's a crucial stepping-stone. If a man asks you to meet his

parents, siblings, etc., and you accept, it's sort of a show of good faith that you both intend to keep each other around.

5. Finally, I need to be in love—real heart-thumping, honest-to-goodness love. I can't allow my boys to fall in love with a man before I do.

Brandi's

IF HIS PROFESSION INVOLVES STANDING ON A BOARD, HE SHOULDN'T BE LYING IN YOUR BED. #SURFERS.

Tweet-ism

9

I'm Just
Not That into You

DUMPED (VERB)

The act of breaking up with your partner in a cruel or particularly thoughtless manner.

Example: Barbie found out she had been dumped when she saw that Ken had updated his Facebook status to single.

Apparently, when you're learning how to date again, it's kind of important that you know how to break up with someone too. Maybe this seems silly, but I've never actually broken up with someone. My first attempt was on camera for *Housewives*, and you probably saw how that turned out. #Disaster. Even when it came to calling things off with a close friend, we somehow avoided *actual* conversations until we both felt normal about things again.

I propose that someone develop a "breakup" app. The Internet is riddled with websites to help you *find* a partner, but I really think we could all use a little assistance when kicking his or her ass to the curb. How about no-match .com or ebreakup.com? Instead of Grinder, how about DumpHer? I would totally create one myself if I knew a damn thing about developing a fucking app—or really anything about technology, computers, or smart phones.

The breakup app of my dreams would have recorded voice memos in different fabulous European accents announcing a variety of reasons that you are breaking up with the person. It would include "We need to talk"; "It's not you, it's me"; "I'm jealous of whoever you end up with"; and other clichéd one-liners. Maybe you could personalize an avatar so that it looks remotely like you. After that, all you have to do is enter your former love interest's e-mail address, and boom! Case closed. Nobody today likes to have actual human contact, unless it involves some kind of oral sex.

The website MissNowMrs.com helps newly married women through the tedious process of legally changing their name. #NeverAgain! I didn't have a website to help guide me, and it was a fucking process. Changing it back was even more of a nightmare. How about a website called AttachedNowSingle.com? It could offer users useful advice about blocking your ex's phone number so he or she can't call you—or so you can't drunk-dial him or her late on a Saturday night. It could walk you through blocking him or her on social media and even track your former partner's iPhone so you can avoid accidental run-ins at local restaurants. I might be on to something here! #StillNeedMy OwnIsland. (I'd at least like to own a house.)

It's like that old song says: breaking up really *is* hard to do. Not just because it hurts or because you might miss the other person, but because in today's world it's actually difficult to get rid of the douche! Douches are meant to stream into the body to cleanse and make the recipient feel good—but they are also meant to stream out of the body. (Read between the lines, guys: get in and then get the fuck out.)

When I get over a guy, I usually just go radio silent. It's totally the coward's way out, but despite what my reality TV alter ego might suggest, I really do hate confrontations of any sort. To be fair, that's only when I'm backing out of what I call "microrelationships" (not significant enough to be dubbed a boyfriend, but not as meaningless as a simple booty call). The more significant relationships I've had should actually have required some sort of breakup conversation—but nope, not me . . . radio silent. Except the

Unicorn Chaser (you'll learn about him in chapter 11). He didn't even deserve radio silence. True story: my boys downloaded *emojis* onto my iPad (I'm still not 100 percent sure of what they are), and I thought it would be funny to use them to break up via e-mail with this guy who I suspected was using me to gain fucking Twitter followers and for other selfish reasons. Since most respectable publishing houses (like mine) haven't yet incorporated *emojis* into their printing capabilities (#GetOnBoard!), I will describe said e-mail: Colorful Hand-Holding Couple, Addition Sign, Tiny Lit Bomb, Addition Sign, Broken Pink Heart, Equals Sign, Fabulous Salsa Dancer Girl, and a Thumbs-Up. He e-mailed me back almost immediately, "What the fuck is this?" I'm still an *emoji* novice, so I decided to revert to my tried-and-true method: radio silence. Then I went and got my nails done. It clearly wasn't love if I was worried more about my stripper nails than his feelings.

I'm a fucking rock star at giving advice (ask any of my friends), but I'm fucking terrible at following it myself. I always know what someone *should* do in a given situation. I just never do it.

In the spirit of "do as I say, not as I do," here I offer my guide to successfully breaking up with a person you no longer want to see naked.

If you're the person doing the breaking up:

1. *Show some respect.* Unless you live on opposite sides of the country (and if you do, this was never going to work anyway) or it was a casual hookup, you should break up in person. Sure, it's harder, but your former partner deserves it. It's the right thing to do. I've actually only tried it once myself, and it didn't go so well. #Hypocrite. #RHOBH. It's easy to send a text or just evaporate into thin air, but that's the coward's way out and it's not fair to leave the other person wondering, "What the fuck just happened?" #DoAsISay. #NotAsIDo.

2. *No ex sex!* The "one more time" theory is great . . . in theory. If you're breaking up with someone who has legitimate feelings for you, fucking one last time is only going to give him or her false hope. Grow some balls and walk away for real. It's never right to waste anyone's time with false hope. You need to let him or her move on. However, if this person was simply a "fuck buddy" to begin with, then by all means keep him or her in the friend box because you never know when you might want a booty call again. (See, I told you. My opinions can change overnight.)

3. *Don't ask to be friends.* At least not right away—especially if it was a lengthy relationship. You need to give your former partner time to move forward—unless of course, he or she has a fancy beach club membership and it's the middle of summer (which would of course mean that I would be waiting until September to break up with him). Then you should definitely try to remain friendly.

4. *Be honest but kind.* Spare this person all the reasons it didn't work out. Your former partner doesn't need to hear that he or she was boring in bed or got too clingy or, worse, that you met someone else. In order to cope, he or she is going to create a mental laundry list of all the reasons you were an undeserving asshole—no need to add to it.

5. *If you got it, don't flaunt it.* If you do decide to remain friends on social media, refrain from posting any pictures of you enjoying your new-found singlehood. Even though you may have already found the hottest new thing in town to hook up with, don't post a picture of the two of you chugging a bottle of expensive champagne.

It just makes you look like a douche bag—and
may scare away the new love interest. I think
there should be a few weeks' grace period before
you post, tweet, or Instagram about someone
new. It's sort of unfair to everyone involved.
#DrewCarter. Even if you didn't just break up
with someone, posting a picture like that is still a
no-no. Keep everybody guessing. #KeepItSexy.

On the flip side of this coin, there is a way to accept
breakups as graciously as possible as an adult. While I like
to think I did the best I could during my divorce, there
were a few (read: many) moments where I allowed my
temper to get the best of me. Learn from my mistakes, so
you can have a better chance of walking away from an
unhealthy situation with your head held high—making
sure your former partner gets a good view of your cute ass
when you leave his or her life forever. Getting dumped
blows; all you can control is how you react. (Speaking of
blowing, you better be doing plenty of it—otherwise that's
probably why your partner is breaking up with you.)

If you're the person being broken up with:

1. *Have a little dignity.* Even if you left your pride
on your bedroom floor, you need to fake it till
you make it. Most dating experts will tell you it's

natural to cry or lash out. Perhaps you have the great idea to slash a car tire—or four. I'm here to tell you that if you leave without breaking down, the other person will immediately question if he or she made the right decision. If someone is crushing you, the worst thing you can do is show him or her how devastated you are. Don't throw a pity party. Take it on the fucking chin, go to the nearest mall, buy yourself the hottest pair of heels you can afford, and wear them out to dinner with all your hottest friends (because you're only as hot as you roll). #Winning.

2. *Disappear.* It's true that absence makes the heart grow fonder, so don't let this douche bag have any access or insight into your life. You might be tempted to post super-hot pictures of yourself in barely there bikinis to your Facebook or Twitter account, but resist the urge! #BeenThere. #DoneThat. He or she will know why you're doing it—especially since I outed most of us in my first book, *Drinking and Tweeting.* It sort of defeats the purpose of going away—even if you do look super-sexy. Never, ever "de-friend" this person, because you are better than he or she is. De-friending someone is the equivalent of

throwing a temper tantrum because your daddy won't take you for ice cream. Friending, de-friending, blocking: It's so fucking lame that this shit is something we even have to worry about nowadays. There's someone better out there, so fuck the guy or girl who left.

3. *Stop the communication.* You may be tempted to drunk-dial him or her after a glass, or in my case a bottle, of white wine. But don't do it! Just say no to your fourth viewing of *The Notebook*, because you know better. It's a bad fucking idea. Also, don't return any texts, e-mails, or calls. This person *broke up* with you—why would you want to talk to him or her? I've heard plenty of girls say, "I don't want him to think I hate him" or "I don't want to be rude." Take it from me: be fucking rude. I always say, "Well, he was rude to you the moment he broke your heart and didn't realize how very special you are." Otherwise, you look desperate. #NotHot. Plus, the longer you ignore them, the sooner they'll start clawing to get you back into their lives.

4. *Medicate!* Now, this may not be necessary for all breakups, but if you're truly struggling, you may

need to seek some outside assistance. For the life of me, I'll never understand the stigma associated with therapy, antidepressants, and antianxiety drugs. Seeing a shrink is the best way to talk out your feelings and get some healthy advice on the best way to move the fuck on. At the very least, it allows you one hour where you can speak out loud without being interrupted by "friends" who only want to chime in to unload their own heartbreak stories—which always feels a little like a competition. Most importantly, if they're licensed psychiatrists, they can also write you a prescription for an antidepressant (my go-to is Lexapro!) or an antianxiety drug to help you move along the therapy train.

5. *Get out of the house.* The worst possible thing for you is to sit around and feel sorry for yourself. I know, because I did it myself for two whole years—and it was miserable. Keeping yourself occupied is the best coping mechanism around. Bury yourself in a new hobby, like redecorating your bedroom. You need to cleanse yourself of the past, and this will make enjoying new experiences with new partners that much easier. Ditching the flower photograph you bought at

Target that you stared at every time your ex got you off is a must. Buy yourself a brand-new mattress, redesign the layout of your bedroom, paint the walls a different color, and update that wall art, yo. Looking at the same shit every morning and every night that you did when you shared your bed with your former partner is a total mind fuck. After that, start training for a marathon or start fucking the hot guy you met at your local bar. (I said it before: the best way to get over someone is to get it on with super-hot, sexy guys!). If all else fails, think of all the new wrinkles you'll avoid getting by not crying over someone who was never going to be worth it anyway.

Brandi's

SERIOUSLY, IF ANYONE CAN HELP ME DEVELOP A BREAKUP APP, TWEET ME @BRANDIGLANVILLE!

Tweet-ism

10

Drinking and Tweeting Again

TWEE-HAB (NOUN)

A facility specializing in caring for men and women who have developed an unhealthy dependency on social media.

Example: After an unsettling month obsessing over the comments of strangers near and far, the country music singer decided to admit herself to a Los Angeles–area twee-hab facility where she met others who also struggled with expressing themselves in 140 characters or less.

@God, help us all. Social media is ruining our lives— one post, tweet, and status update at a time. But like most people, I can't seem to stop myself!

Okay, so let me start by making amends for yet another instance where I stuck my foot in my big mouth: I take back what I said about twee-hab. I know I laughed social media addiction off as a fictional disorder invented by someone who couldn't stop obsessively stalking an ex online, but social media *can* be a real addiction.

In my defense, it did sound like total bullshit at first. Seriously, who really has to be admitted into a treatment facility for exhaustion or stress therapy because they can't stop refreshing their Twitter feed? Apparently, a lot of people do.

I'm not sure if actual twee-hab centers already exist, but they absolutely should. If not, I'll be the genius to open the very first one—and become a fucking billionaire!

I firmly believe that it's the newest form of cutting for bored suburban housewives and singles. Regardless of who or what you're obsessing over, it can quickly become all-consuming and totally self-indulgent. Some people post "selfies" of their new haircut so their followers can agree that their game-time decision to cut their bangs was a good one. Some parents obsessively post pictures of their kids in the bathtub, with captions like "Jenny loves bubble beards!" I'm a mom, so I understand that you think your children are the cutest ones in the world and that you want to share that cuteness with everyone on Facebook. What I don't understand is the kiddy porn. These lines should not

be crossed, people! Put your son or daughter in some cho-
nies or a bathing suit. There are perverts in the world!
When it comes to Twitter, twit-aholics are just obsessed
with what everyone else is talking about—or if other
people care about what *they* are talking about. If that
weren't true, then why else would people tweet?

My social media addiction escalated from casually scroll-
ing through my news feed a few times a day or searching
for people I had met around town to a full-fledged dependency. I think a Twittervention may have been and still
may be in order.

Twitter was my gateway drug to an alternate reality—
which included Facebook and now Instagram (although
tweeting still remains my favorite high). The more I engaged with my followers and the people I was following—
both positively and negatively—the more I needed it.
#BlockTheHaters. It's like a parallel universe where you
can meet new people, live vicariously through the fabulous
and famous, connect with old friends, and obsess over
those who are no longer in your life. Between my smart
phone, my iPad, and my laptop, I had access to social
media 24/7.

In my first book, I was candid about using social
media—and Google alerts—to obsess over my ex-husband
and his new life. Sure, I was "addicted," but I rationalized
that Twitter-stalking was the only way to find out what

my children were doing since he and I communicated solely through his assistant. When my eldest son went to the hospital with an injury after a sleepover, I only found out once his bonus mom sent out a Tweet. It seemed insane that I wouldn't even be notified that my baby was in the hospital, but that was the reality also known as my life.

Our coparenting hasn't really improved much, but Mason has a new cell phone, which I pay for so that I actually have a shot at reaching my kids when they're not with me (but it's not like a ten-year-old remembers to charge the damn thing or where it is). Nowadays, I'm no longer interested in my ex-husband's life with his new wife—other than how it relates to my boys—so religiously checking her news feed no longer interests me. Plus, her passive-aggressive tweets are kind of lame.

My online addiction evolved into a three-pronged obsession (and I only participate in the three core social media platforms: Twitter, Facebook, and now Instagram). I can't even begin to wrap my head around Vine, Foursquare, Klout, or Tumblr. First, it was a way for me to connect with my supporters and fans of the television show . . . and even the shit talkers. Reading words of encouragement helped brighten some of my gloomiest days. It also gave me a place to respond to all the cowards who hide behind "egg-shaped" icons and create accounts purely to talk trash. These people are cowards and losers.

Next I had a constant need to see what people were talking about in cyberspace (#TheRoyalBaby, #North West, #BreakingBad, and, of course, what's going on in my own life).

Finally, given my new commitment to be open to love again, I used Twitter and Facebook to begin investigating just about every guy I considered dating and to keep tabs on the ones I'd long since kicked to the curb. It's essentially *Stalking for Dummies* and, therefore, the most dangerous tool in the modern dating world.

Gone are the days when the "three-day rule" actually applied. #Totally90s. Between texts, tweets, and Facebook messages, there are no excuses.

Let's just start with simple cell phones: technology makes it virtually impossible to pretend you didn't get the voice mail or see the text message. I don't know any normal person who goes more than a day without checking his or her cell, so either fucking respond or go away. On certain phones, you can even see if your message has been delivered and read. If you have time to read it, you have time to send a reply—unless someone sends you an out-of-the-blue text that says "Hey" or "Sup," in which case he doesn't want to date you, he just wants to make sure you're still interested in case he ever wants to fuck you again.

When a day or two passes and you still don't get a response, your mind starts to wander. Is he playing games with me? Maybe she doesn't want to talk to me anymore? Did he find someone else he's more interested in? If you're like me, you realize you're being a fucking lunatic and tell yourself to calm down. I'm sure he's just really busy. Or is he? #MindFuck.

Welcome to the curse of social media. After a glass or two of your favorite wine, you may decide to check his Twitter feed or her Facebook page and see that person has more than enough time to retweet a story about the Knicks or post some lame e-card (whatever that is) about hating Mondays. He or she has time for that, but no time to respond to a fucking message? Or, worse, he says, "I'm staying in tonight," but posts a picture on Instagram from the bar at the Sunset Tower. #Idiot. I fucking hate liars.

Like I said, it's easy to obsess. But be warned, it's just as easy for him or her to find out what you're doing, so use this to your advantage! Let the games begin.

After nine months of back and forth, my Latin boyfriend and I were "on" again—at least for the night anyway. The boys were with their dad, and I was sitting home alone, feeling in need of a little TLC and slightly sorry for myself, so I sent him a text: "Sup." (I too am guilty of using this. Just like the people who have used it on me, it's a safe bet. That way, if he doesn't respond, you didn't really put yourself out there.) He quickly replied back with an

eager "Hi. How are you? You've been on my mind."
#Sucker.

We engaged in a little "small text." He asked if I had the boys that evening—it was his way of gauging how available I was and if he had a chance of getting laid that night, and the answer was, yes, he did.

"No, and I feel like cooking Stroganoff," I responded after a few minutes (always leave them hanging, just a little bit). Like my mom always says, the way to any man's heart is with a home-cooked meal. And like *I* always say, a braless tank top should take care of the rest. He arrived around seven P.M. with a bottle of wine and a smile. I felt relieved. He seemed to be in a good mood, so I thought I would dodge any drawn-out chats about why we were on yet another break, a conversation he seemed to want to have repeatedly. (He was seriously more sensitive than *any* woman I've ever met.)

He poured himself a glass of wine (not me), plopped himself down on a bar stool at my kitchen counter as I chopped vegetables, and immediately pulled out his iPhone. We spent the next two hours dissecting my every tweet and Facebook status update (even though I've told him that I rarely use Facebook anymore). I've repeatedly told him that I never talk about my love interests on social media (although I totally do), hoping that it would save me from having this exact conversation. He began reciting things I posted during our "breakup" and demanding explanations. Really, dude? "I saw the 'men are babies' post," he said, as he sat across from me and sipped his wine (or should I say "whine"). "What was that about?"

I wasn't prepared for the third degree. Was he going to usher me into an interrogation room and force me under a glaring light? Did he want to handcuff me and rough me up? I might have been into that, actually, but without the interrogation.

"I have two sons," I said, standing over the stove and focusing on sautéing the peppers. "And truth be told, all men *are* babies."

Of course that was true, but the post was actually about a full-blown freak-out my Unicorn Chaser had when I said in an interview that I had a New York boyfriend, but it didn't matter because my L.A. boyfriend seemed to be buying it.

"What about the 'just say no to actors' tweet?" he asked. Finally, I relented and poured myself a glass of wine. Didn't he know what he was here for? I wasn't trying to get back together. I wanted to use him for sex! I finally know what men feel like. I had a stage 5 clinger! He was going to use this opportunity to torture me. This was going to be a long night . . . and not in a fun way.

"My ex-husband was an actor," I shrugged, before adding with a flirty smile: "I feel like I should warn people." This explanation didn't seem to go over as smoothly. "Fine," I relented. "An actor recently asked me out and I turned him down." It was 100 percent true, and I figured he might feel a little vindicated by this.

However, the post he was referring to was about a gorgeous African American actor I dated for a few months long before I ever met the Latino, who had recently hit me up again. #Sup. (See chapter 4.)

Before I continue I have to reveal that I'm a *terrible* liar. These half-truths were the only way I could tap-dance around his accusations. I didn't want to lie to him. I pride myself on being honest. I've learned the hard way that lying gets you nowhere, but on this particular night I just needed him to stop. I was willing to fudge the truth a little so we could get it on.

It's not like we were in a committed relationship anyway! He knew I was dating other people and I knew he was dating other people, but for my own sanity, I chose not to stalk his Facebook wall. So why was he torturing himself? And more importantly, why was he torturing me? I tried to remember if the sex was even good enough for me to subject myself to this. (It was.)

By this time, dinner was ready and we sat on opposite ends of my glass table. The wine was kicking in, and I was calming down. Honestly, I was hoping that the bickering and jealousy might have turned him on. We could pretend that it would be our "last time" (even though we both knew it wouldn't be), because it would make the sex that much more intense and passionate.

But my Latino just kept his eyes fixated on his phone, as if he were conjuring up more questions to hurl at me. *Come on,* I thought. I just wanted to eat, then get fucked. I mean, I wasn't asking for much. And seriously, what hot-blooded American man turns down a home-cooked meal followed by hot, steamy sex?

I understood torturing yourself with jealousy can be a super-sexy form of foreplay, but this shit was getting ridiculous—and seriously fucking annoying.

"Remember that night you cancelled our dinner at Craig's because you weren't feeling well?" he asked. I nodded. "Well, why did you post later that you were going to 'stay up and out all night'?"

That was the final straw. "Enough!" I shouted, slamming my wineglass a little too ferociously on the counter. (I didn't want to waste perfectly good wine.) He wasn't even right at this point. Those were two completely different evenings.

"Were you seriously just sitting at home and checking my Twitter all night, every night?" I demanded.

"No!" he shouted. "My friend sent it to me the next day. He knew we were supposed to go out, so he wanted to know what we did."

"Bullshit," I said. Yep, I was calling it. He was trying to make me feel guilty for something I didn't actually do. I knew 100 percent that I *did* stay in that night.

Calmly, I explained that sometimes I just type things into my little phone for fun—like when I go to bed at nine P.M. with my little men and want people (specifically future boyfriends) to think that I'm out and about at the most fabulous, exclusive party that none of them got invites to (because it wasn't fucking real).

It's true. When I'm feeling boring or particularly lame, I occasionally post shit so I sound more fabulous than I am. I don't do it often, but it makes other people happy and, oddly, me too. I don't consider it a "lie" because I'm not telling anyone in particular. But on that specific night I was fast asleep after two glasses of Whispering Angel and some NyQuil.

His interrogation continued well through dinner, but I hoped that by calling him a "cyberstalker" that I had shamed him enough so he would stop checking up on me . . . or at least not bother me about it if he did. By the time the dishes were done, I told him I had a headache and was going to crash. And yes, after three hours of this badgering, I did actually have a headache. He playfully asked if I wanted company. *Oh*, I thought, *of course* now *he's in the mood to get frisky.*

"No, thanks," I said. "Call me crazy, but I'm not really in the mood anymore."

As soon as his car pulled out of the driveway, I took to my Twitter.

"Headed to Polo Lounge with my #BFFs!"

It was one of those rare nights when I turned off my phone and shut down my iPad. I curled up on my couch with the rest of the wine and watched *Pretty Woman* before falling asleep.

Here are my rules for being a responsible social media citizen, version 2.0:

1. If an anonymous person who hides behind a fake account and a default profile picture is trashing you, do yourself a favor and click "Block." This will save you hours of useless agonizing and help you avoid becoming embroiled in a #TwitterWar.

2. Cyberbullying is an actual epidemic that is scary and very real. If you're a middle-aged woman receiving a barrage of nasty comments from some assholes, you're not being bullied. You're just dealing with assholes.

3. Limit yourself to uploading only one photo of your child per day. I know that your son was the first child to ever get his face painted at the fair, but please try to control yourself. And never under any circumstances post a sonogram photo. That shit's just weird. #SorryButISaidIt.

4. If you're going to post a "selfie," do so with caution. Always tilt the camera slightly downward and, please, flip the fucking phone around. Seeing the flash reflect in the bathroom mirror and your toilet in the background is not hot. #LearnFromMyMistakes.

5. Also, enough with posting pictures of the food you're eating and meticulously describing each ingredient. It just makes me hungry, and that makes me not like you. #FoodPorn.

6. Restrain yourself from oversharing about a bad breakup. That's a surefire way to send any future dating prospects running in the opposite

direction—and your friends get tired of hearing about it. Trust me, I know. #GuiltyAsCharged.

7. Stop "checking in" at the gym on Facebook or Foursquare. (But really, who still uses Foursquare?) If you have a bangin' body, I'm sure you've posted enough bathing suit pictures for everyone to know.

8. Getting a public figure to respond to your shitty comments on Twitter doesn't make you look cool. It just makes you look like you don't have a life.

9. Regardless of privacy settings, remember that all social media is essentially public. Any of your followers can screen-grab your photos, updates, and direct messages. If you want to share something you wouldn't want your mother to see, it's probably not a good idea to post it. My mom, actually, does not participate in social media. #ThankGod.

10. And finally, an oldie but a goodie: above all, don't drink and tweet. #StillAHypocrite.

Brandi's

TWEET A FABULOUS PICTURE
OF YOURSELF AND TAG THE
COOLEST RESTAURANT IN TOWN,
THEN PUT ON A HYDRATING
FACE MASK AND PRETEND TO
BE UNAVAILABLE.

Tweet-ism

11

The Unicorn Chaser

UNICORN (NOUN)

1. A mythical female creature without flaw; the perfect ten.

2. A figment of the male imagination.

Example: The Wall Street financier wanted a unicorn: a girl with all-natural bouncy blond hair; a perfect bikini bod; a Harvard education; an in-depth knowledge of MLB, NFL, NHL, and NBA; an endless trust fund; a mouth like a sailor; and a perfect pink pussy. Oh, and she can cook too.

He was attractive, just not my particular brand of attractive.

Not long after my fresh start in the dating world, my best friend Amy wanted to set me up with this guy she knew. He was a successful New York television producer in his midthirties and was renting a summerhouse in Malibu with some friends—a group of committed bachelors. (This should have been my first warning sign, but I was a sucker for beachfront real estate.) I had been on a handful of blind dates and I wasn't really itching to go on another one, but Amy was persistent. Plus, I hadn't been having the best luck on my own (my picker was off, for sure), so I finally conceded, but I wasn't going to make it easy. I half hoped I might dissuade him altogether.

The sun was still shining when I forced him to pick me up at my rental in The Valley—about an hour's drive for anyone coming from the coast. To be clear, I rarely let a guy pick me up on the first date (after all, it's only a few steps from the driveway to the bedroom), but I already decided that this wasn't going anywhere. I even warned him that my babysitter could only stay a short time, so I had a strict eight P.M. curfew. (The boys were actually with their dad. #BigFatLie.) I suggested we go to a sushi restaurant near my house, which just so happened to be in a strip mall. I was so over the date entirely that I threw on jeans and a T-shirt—I mean, they were definitely fitted jeans and there might have been a little nipple action under the shirt, but it was still jeans and a T-shirt. I even wore flats. I haven't worn flats on a date since . . . well, ever.

Needless to say, this wasn't the makings of a super-sexy first date. It was just another stepping-stone, I told myself.

He pulled up in a black SUV that he borrowed from a friend—which made me wonder if he was moonlighting as an Uber driver. The one-mile car ride to the strip mall sushi joint was already uncomfortable. I quickly realized we had nothing in common besides our mutual friends and the fact that we both worked in television. Was this essentially a glorified business meeting? I wasn't sure.

Walking into the restaurant, I noticed he had a beanie in the back pocket of his jeans. There are *so* many things wrong with that picture. It's like, "Come on, dude. You're a thirty-something-year-old businessman. Why would you ever need to wear a beanie?" And did I mention that it was June . . . in Los Angeles? I decided it must be his version of a security blanket—or, more likely, to cover up the bald spot on the back of his head.

When we were finally seated, I immediately ordered a glass of white wine, thinking that maybe a little alcohol would loosen us up. He ordered a glass of water. *Fuck me*, I thought—and not in the good way. I squawked on about my job and my kids as he sat there rocking a pimp lean. You know the one—where his left leg is straight out to the side and his right elbow is leaning across the table. It dawned on me that this guy seriously thought he was gangsta. I wanted to say, "Honey, you're not Jay-Z. You're a New York Jew." (Ironically, this is why I eventually fell head over heels for him . . . or so I thought.)

After I drained my second glass of wine, I was waiting for my booze goggles to click on, but they never did—which I have to admit is pretty unusual for me. The dinner lasted about forty-five minutes (I would eventually learn that nothing lasts longer than a few minutes with this dude), and I glanced down at the watch I wasn't wearing and announced, "Well, I have to go."

It was still light outside when we pulled up to my house well before my self-imposed curfew. "Can I come in?" he asked. Men rarely surprise me anymore, but what about that incredibly awkward forty-five-minute date caused him to believe that there was any chance that I would let him into my house where he believed my kids were? I mean, he didn't know that the house was empty. I thanked him for dinner and leaned over to give him a weird hug/back pat combo before jumping out of the SUV.

I went inside, put on my heels, slapped on some red lipstick, and hit the town. The night was still young.

*I don't remember the first time we had sex. I remem-*ber the car ride to his house, and I remember waking up in his bed with my top still on, but the actual sex? Nope. Not a clue.

But in my defense, I was drunk and alone on Christmas Eve. My children were with their dad for the night (spending the holidays without my boys isn't something I think I'll ever get used to), so I needed something to take my mind off of it. Knowing what I know now, I'm not sure there was much to remember anyway.

After our tragic first date, he started inviting me to the weekly soirees at his Malibu rental. By then, I decided that he was a nice guy; he just wasn't my cup of tea. (I'm actually pretty picky about my tea bags. #TeaBagging. #GetIt?) He was somewhat charming during our phone conversations and witty, but I wasn't really seeing any sparks fly. So while I wasn't necessarily interested in dating him, who was I to turn down a Malibu beach party? He suggested I bring a few girlfriends with me, which I didn't think much of at the time.

When my girlfriends and I got to his not-so-humble abode, it didn't take long for me to figure out why he had invited them: he was a unicorn chaser. He was the kind of guy who had a mental checklist of every unrealistic quality his ideal woman should have. And what was Mr. Beanie in His Back Pocket's particular flavor of unicorn? A quick-witted twenty-something Victoria's Secret model with an MBA (and that's just the tip of the iceberg). So he and his friends would pack their parties with tall, leggy women who they could pick and choose from before ultimately dissecting. He knew that I met most of my closest friends while modeling, so it was a pretty safe assumption that whomever I brought to the party would also fit this mold.

If that wasn't another red fucking flag to send me in the opposite direction, the beanbag chair, zebra hide rug, and motherfucking water bed surely should have sent me running. A water bed? Really? These grown-ass men fell into some money and were living out the equivalent of a nineties-themed bachelor pad. I didn't know whether they'd be serving wine or charging for keg cups. Was someone going to Sharpie an "X" on my hand? Were we going to play quarters? Or maybe beer pong? Actually, I don't even know what beer pong is, but I'm sure the twenty-two-year-olds did.

At first I was totally disgusted, but then I was surprisingly flattered. His laundry list of ex-girlfriends could pretty much double as the *Sports Illustrated* swimsuit issue, and he wanted to date me: a thirty-eight-year-old mother of two. I do have the vagina of a seventeen-year-old (or maybe more like a twenty-three-year-old now), so I guess it averages out. #NewKitty.

We didn't start sleeping together immediately. In fact, it took about eighteen months before our Christmas Eve blackout sex. That summer I actually dated a few of the Unicorn Chaser's friends—including one who was a pretty famous movie star (just google it)—but he and I would spend a lot of time together just trading jabs and goofing around and actually developed something of a friendship. He would offer me career advice, and I tried desperately to talk him out of wearing True Religion jeans. And beyond the fact of having nothing to talk about on our sushi date nightmare, I discovered we actually had a very similar sense of humor and would start beating each other to the punch line of a joke. My interest was slowly starting to rise—despite his ever-present beanie. Whenever I went to one of his parties, he would get drunk and tell me how "into me" he was, and without fail, two minutes later I would see him off in a corner with some other girl.

It only made me *more* interested.

When September rolled around and my Unicorn Chaser headed back to New York, he and I would have weekly phone dates where we would catch up on everything going on. It became a routine and I looked forward to it, but still nothing physical ever happened between us. He was clever enough to subtly drop the name of a girl he was seeing into the conversation, always some twenty-something model type, making it abundantly clear that beyond his mother, I was the oldest woman in his life. We would see each other whenever we were both in the same city, but always in a group environment, so I wouldn't confuse it with a date. For someone who wanted me as desperately as he claimed to, he never wanted to actually be alone with me. Even if he asked me to meet him for a drink at the Beverly Hills Hotel, he would have a buddy there. He was the king of the backup plan. (One more time for the cheap seats: red flag.)

The following summer, the Unicorn Chaser was back in Malibu at his nineties bachelor pad beach house. (Seriously, where was Brandon Walsh? Or even David Silver?) He invited me over for a party (translation: with his friends and about twenty model-looking girls in bikinis) and spent the entire afternoon flirting with other women right in front of me. And guess what? It worked. Seeing him get all this attention from hot young women made me want to devour him. It had been nearly a year of buildup and home girl was ready!

I begged my friend to stay with me while the party started to wind down. Getting my Unicorn Chaser alone was going to be a challenge, so I needed to enlist her help! #DesperateTimes. And like any quality wing woman, she agreed to make out with his friend . . . on the beanbag chair. #TrueFriend. I knew damn well that there was no real future with this guy, but when have I made smart decisions when it comes to guys? Besides maybe divorcing one.

With my friend fully engaged in a tenth-grade heavy petting session on the beanbag chair, I excused myself and headed toward the kitchen, hopeful that my Unicorn Chaser would follow me. I knew what I wanted, but he was going to have to come to me. I was pouring myself another glass of wine when I heard someone behind me. I spun around expecting to see my Unicorn Chaser, but it wasn't him. It was one of the model groupies who had been flirting with him—and me—all night.

"Who makes this?" she asked, rubbing the side of my waist.

"Cavalli," I said, not quite sure what to do but not hating the attention. She leaned in to kiss me, and I thought, *Why not?* If my Unicorn Chaser wasn't going to give me any action, I might as well get some from the hot twenty-something model. #WaistUpLesbian.

We were in a full-blown make-out session when my Unicorn Chaser finally found us in the kitchen.

"Oh," he said, sounding surprised and amused at the same time. The groupie girl was clearly a little embarrassed and excused herself immediately, which meant I was finally alone with my Unicorn Chaser. He was so turned on that he walked right up to me and kissed me. I guess seeing *me* flirt with the hot, sexy models made him want me too.

We made our way down to the cold, hard marble kitchen floor as his hand made its way up my dress. I immediately thought about how disgusting the floor was and how expensive my dress was. Did I like him more than my dress? But before I could react, I felt a few of his fingers find their way inside. #ShockerStyle. While it wasn't the incredible make-out session I hoped it would be, it wasn't completely unenjoyable. After a few minutes, he pulled his tongue out of my mouth and whispered, "It's getting late."

Just like that, I lost whatever power I had. The dynamic had completely shifted, and I gave Mr. Beanie in His Back Pocket total control.

"Yeah, you're right," I muttered, not quite sure how to handle the situation.

"I'll call you guys a car," he said. At least he was offering to send us home in a town car; it *was* the gentlemanly thing to do, after all. He spent the last twelve months trying to get down my pants, and here he was with two fingers up my kitty cat and he's rejecting me? Are you fucking serious? #FuckOff. Something about me that night wasn't meeting his standards, and it made me want him even more. #FuckMe.

Five minutes later, a yellow cab—not a town car— appeared in front of the Malibu beach house to drive my girlfriend and me home. I paid.

"There's been an accident," I said. My Latino boyfriend was ten minutes away, and I needed an excuse to flake. We had been dating casually for about six months, and I had offered to make him his favorite home-cooked meal. I was

sipping a glass of white wine (#DrinkingAndCooking) and chopping green onions, bell peppers, and mushrooms when my Unicorn Chaser called. He was staying at a friend's house in Bel Air and wanted to see a movie with me.

"It's my, um, cousin," I lied through my teeth. "I already ordered a cab to the airport."

It was a horrible thing to do, but I hadn't seen the Unicorn Chaser in months, and this sounded like an actual date. The Latino said that he was already down the street and would come help me.

"I'll drive you to the airport," he offered.

"No, the cab is already on the way," I said, before adding, "but if you could watch the dogs that would be awesome." If I spent the night with the Unicorn Chaser, it would be helpful if my Latino could watch the dogs. To be fair, the Latino had me jumping through hoops for months. It was his turn to repay the favor.

"Um, okay," he said, begrudgingly. "I'll be there in a few minutes."

Fuck, I thought. I ran into my closet and grabbed my black carry-on Tumi bag with cranberry ribbon and tossed it by the door. I'll tell you this, if I was going to fake an emergency trip to Sacramento for a cousin who wasn't injured, I was going to really commit. Looking back, I should have won an Emmy for my performance. At least someone in my family would have an acting award.

By the time my Latino arrived, I was putting the chopped vegetables in Tupperware.

"Don't worry about it," he said, clearly annoyed, but attempting to understand. "I'll take care of it." The creases in his ear lobes were really starting to bother me. I know how insane that must sound, but I couldn't stop staring at them as he pouted over the sink. So I did what any girl would do: I faked a phone call from my mom and pretended to cry.

The cab had arrived, and the Latino grabbed my empty suitcase to carry to the car.

"This is really light," he said.

"I'm only going for a night," I quickly snapped, praying to God that he didn't think to open it. I really was planning to be back by morning. I jumped in the cab; I was almost there. I yelled at the driver, "Yo, homes, to Bel Air." #FreshPrinceRules.

I pulled up to a ridiculous mansion about ten minutes later and hid my bag to the side of the front steps; I didn't want to give him the satisfaction of knowing I made an excuse to see him. I rang the bell, and his friend answered the door. Apparently, this was going to be a double date.

By the time we got to the theater, I was starved. I hadn't eaten all day, and I had planned to be eating beef Stroganoff by now. My Latino had already texted me that he locked up the house and wished me a safe flight. #ImGoingToHell.

"I'm going to get a hot dog," I announced. He seemed totally annoyed that I was ordering food. Was I not allowed to eat? I dressed my hot dog with ketchup, mustard, and tons of relish.

"Who puts relish on a hot dog?" he asked, looking totally disgusted. Apparently, unicorns don't eat relish.

"I do," I responded, taking a big bite of my kosher dog. Despite his feigned repulsion, I thought that it wouldn't be my only wiener that night.

I had no idea what we were even seeing, but when the opening credits rolled, the headlining name was a familiar one—to both of us. I was totally confused. Why would he take me to see a movie starring his friend who I had hooked up with?

I realized that he wanted to get jealous. Knowing that I hooked up with the guy on the big movie screen was turning him on. He spent the entire movie playing high school grab ass with me—rubbing my leg and holding my hand. I was just waiting for the fake yawn when he would put his arm around me. And yes, in some twisted way I was really into it.

After the movie, I had no less than ten text messages from the Latino asking if I landed safely. "Yes," I quickly typed. "At hospital. Can't talk." (I realize that if he's reading this now, he's probably pretty pissed. So let me say it here: #ImSoSorry.)

When we got back to the Bel Air house, my Unicorn Chaser and I went immediately to the bedroom. I was ready for an evening filled with crazy, hot sex, but we ended up snuggling the entire night. It felt intimate and sweet. Or maybe it was that my breath still smelled like relish. Either way, I was okay with it.

The next morning, I grabbed my empty suitcase and went home, thoroughly confused.

My Unicorn Chaser was back in Los Angeles during the holidays, but I hadn't seen him yet. We kept up our regular phone calls and e-mails but never talked about what happened on the kitchen floor or the movie theater. I knew he was dating other people and he knew I was as well, but neither of us brought it up. When you ask that question, everyone loses. Plus, we weren't in a relationship, but clearly *something* was going on, I just had no clue what. I knew he was attracted to me, but at the end of the day, I was just too old to be his unicorn. And I liked relish.

I was spending Christmas Eve with my L.A. family: Yolanda and David Foster. They were gracious enough to invite me to dinner at Yolanda's ex-husband's mansion in Beverly Hills. While I don't ever anticipate having a blended holiday dinner with my ex-husband anytime soon, I definitely respect the relationship Yolanda was able to maintain with her ex for the sake of their children. We had finished up a gorgeous meal, and people were starting to trickle out. The Unicorn Chaser had already called me earlier in the day, and I told him that I would let him know if my dinner ended early. I was already in a champagne haze, so I decided to see if he wanted to meet for a drink at the Beverly Hills Hotel.

This goes against everything I stand for, but I was alone, and the idea of going home to an empty house on Christmas Eve depressed the shit out of me.

By the time he got to the Polo Lounge, I was pretty tipsy. He had, of course, brought a friend but climbed into the booth next to me. We ordered a round of drinks, and without much hesitation, my hand made its way into his lap. I started feeling him under the table, while he was struggling to pay attention to a story his friend was telling. I kept one elbow perched on the table, with my head in my hand, laughing at all the right moments, while I got him hard underneath the table. #Vulgar. #ButHot.

After a few minutes, I looked at him innocently and said, "Should we go?"

He drove us to the Bel Air palace, and I don't remember much after that, except that I woke up a few hours later with just my pants off. He had already called a cab, which was waiting outside for me. I took the ten-minute cab ride back to my house alone. I paid. #FullCircle.

•••

The next time I fucked the Unicorn Chaser, it wasn't much more memorable.

I was in New York for work about two months after our Christmas Eve encounter, and he invited me out to dinner.

"If it's going to be a group date, I'm not really interested," I said, thinking I was playing it cool. He assured me it wasn't but told me his friend was having dinner at a nearby restaurant and he promised to stop by. Once again, I should have known better but agreed nonetheless.

Cipriani is something of a New York institution. It's an upscale Italian restaurant that's been around for eons with an impressive list of celebrity clientele and Manhattan power players, including Jay-Z, naturally. Basically, you go for the scene, not for the food. When we arrived at the table, there were three beautiful women and one older man and, of course, two empty chairs for the Unicorn Chaser and me. We weren't going to be making our dinner reservation.

I immediately recognized another woman at the table—the ex-girlfriend of a guy I had dated. She recognized me too, but we both played dumb. I settled into my seat and thought, *So much for stopping by.* Not long into my group date dinner, the Unicorn Chaser actually had the balls to start flirting with this other woman right in front of me. After dinner, we made our way to the rooftop nightclub, and I started wondering if he was getting a fucking appearance fee for bringing me there. What the fuck did I sign up for here? #Loser.

I started drinking, dancing, and posing for pictures with other guests when they asked, which he scolded me about later. (Gee, thanks, Dad.) By this point, I wasn't even paying much attention to him and he knew I was annoyed, which, of course, turned him on. He finally asked me if he could take me home.

Now, this applies to most people—as soon as you don't want them, they are suddenly desperate to have you. The Unicorn Chaser was no different.

I crawled into the backseat of a cab and directed the driver to my ultra-sleek downtown hotel in the Meatpacking District. It's basically a "come fuck me" hotel. I wasn't going to let him take me to his Upper East Side apartment; this was going to be on my terms—or so I thought. He slid in next to me and put on his motherfucking beanie. Seriously, dude?

But before I could think too much about it, he grabbed my face and started kissing me. He's not a bad kisser, but he's not the best. By the time we arrived at the hotel, we had found our groove and I was getting into it.

"I'm coming up," he said. It wasn't a question and I didn't appear to have a say in the matter, which totally turned me on. By New York standards, my room was enormous: I had a sitting room, kitchen, and full bedroom. Without invitation, he plopped himself on the couch and turned on SportsCenter. #SuperSexy. I announced that I was going to change into something more comfortable, which meant ripping off my dress and strutting into the living room in my Agent Provocateur lingerie with super-sexy panties. I placed myself on the couch next to him and said, "So?"

Without saying a word, he pulled me on top of him and pushed my G-string to the side. We started kissing and I went for the belt on his jeans. I already had such a strong emotional connection that while the sex wasn't amazing, I was crazy turned on. I was on top of him on the couch for maybe six minutes before he pushed me off to the side so he could finish himself inside his own jeans. Did I mention that his pants didn't even make their way off his ass? He got up, tucked it in, and left.

I don't have enough space to dissect everything wrong with this picture. For starters, I didn't even get off. The only reason I even entertained the idea was because I figured it would be mutually beneficial. As a woman in her forties, if I'm not getting an orgasm out of the deal, what's the point? This isn't a bullshit twenty-something drunken hookup. We're adults and we all have needs. Let's face it, a girl's got to orgasm. #Right? Okay, fine. For the sake of argument, let's just say the sex was so amazing for him that he couldn't hold out any longer. I won't fault him for that, not totally. But come on, you're a grown-ass man who talks a big fucking game. You should really know how to find a woman's G-spot—or at least make a solid attempt trying to. But at the end of the day, I should at the very least get a little oral action. Fair is fair. Apparently, pussy isn't kosher. #JewishGuys.

So, you can imagine my total shock when he got up to fucking leave. I was stuck horny as fuck in a hotel, thinking, *Well, this sucks.* I may not have had a unicorn horn, but I sure was a thoroughbred. Listen up, boys. Girls need to get off too.

This guy apparently gets twenty-three-year-old hot model pussy and is terrible in bed. How does that work? I was utterly confused as I sat alone in my oversized hotel room in lacy lingerie. But then it hit me—how much did I know about my body, sex, and needs at twenty-three? Not much. That's the kind of wisdom that comes with age and confidence—two things his frequent partners didn't have much of. Plus, I spent more than a decade with the same man exploring our sexuality. For the Unicorn Chaser, his girlfriends were satisfied with a fancy dinner and six minutes of underwhelming sex. Sometimes I'm grateful I'm not twenty-three anymore.

To make matters worse, we didn't use a condom. All ended up fine at my next gynecologist appointment, but I still cringe whenever I think about it. But rest assured, ladies and gays, he had at least one of his heads covered, because he never even took off his fucking beanie.

Much like a snowflake, no two unicorn chasers are the same. Men all have different ideas of their perfect unicorn. However, I have devised this foolproof guide to spotting a potential unicorn chaser in the wild:

1. He lives in a full-service condo or luxury hotel. The unicorn chaser needs to be waited on hand and foot.

2. He never waits in line. The unicorn chaser is the most popular guy in town.

3. He has an impressive list of ex-girlfriends, but his relationships never last longer than a few months.

4. He's an only child. For the unicorn chaser, it's all about me, me, me.

5. He doesn't want children. Once again: me, me, me.

6. He has performance problems in the bedroom. The unicorn chaser doesn't have to fuck like a rock star. He thinks you should feel lucky that he's fucking you at all.

7. He invites you on a date with twenty other people. The unicorn chaser can never have too many options.

8. He brags about all the famous people he knows. If you don't already know how cool the unicorn chaser is, he's going to tell you.

9. He isn't the most attractive guy. Typically, the unicorn chaser spent his adolescence being picked on by the kinds of women he now uses and discards. He's making up for some troubling high school years.

10. He has a house with a water bed. #NuffSaid.

I no longer see the Unicorn Chaser. We still talk on occasion, but I won't ever be his unicorn. I can't make my-self ten years younger, and I can't help that I like relish. I'll probably never go to college, I'll always want orgasms, and I can't un-give birth to my two beautiful sons (although my vagina did). I'll never be perfect, and I don't think I ever want to be. My imperfections are what make me, me. I have realized that I don't any longer want to chase an unattainable man, because I'll never win. He was my first true heartbreak since putting myself out there again. I'm not sure if I loved him, or if I just told myself that I did, but surviving it was important. It showed me just how strong I had become—something I sometimes fail to see.

Heartbreak, failure, and loss are the times I learn the most about myself. It's true that sometimes you need to get up to get down, but occasionally you need to get down to get up.

Brandi's

I DON'T BELIEVE IN UNICORNS, BUT I STILL DESERVE A FAIRY TALE.

Tweet-ism

12

My "In Case of Emergency" Contact

"IN CASE OF EMERGENCY" CONTACT (NOUN)

The ridiculous paper you are forced to fill out at the dermatologist's office when you are just there to get a zit injected that makes you feel like shit because you realize just how alone you are.

Example: Her hand froze as she was filling out the form and came to the dreaded line, "In case of emergency, contact . . ."

Every time I'm at a doctor's appointment, I struggle with the question: "Who should we contact in case of emergency?" For a few years after my divorce, I named my ex-husband's parents. My mom and dad still live in northern California, so I would most likely bleed out before they could make the six-hour drive to Los Angeles. My former in-laws were nearby, and I knew they would be there for me if shit ever *truly* hit the fan. They told me as much. Sadly, though, regardless of their offer, they're not my family anymore, and it doesn't feel appropriate to list them as the people I would depend on if something catastrophic were to occur. My former in-laws will always have a special place in my heart, but no longer a place in my life.

Truthfully, I didn't really know who would show up for me in case of an emergency. I'm sure the doctors' offices didn't intend to send me into a philosophical free fall, but they did—every time. I'm a single mother who does everything for herself. Thankfully, I was forced into becoming this independent woman, and I was proud not having to ask for help, but this silly little question made me feel like absolute shit. Truth be told, I *did* want someone to be responsible for me. But I just hadn't had any luck finding him yet.

I had a few names in my "ICE" rotation: my gaygent Michael, my best friend Trina, and my fake ex-husband Darin. Of course, I know that my friends love me, but they are all busy living their own lives and raising their own families. A lot of times, I would just leave it blank. Seriously, I don't foresee any "emergencies" happening during my facial appointment, unless you count a ridiculous acne breakout or a needle-happy aesthetician (nothing a muscle relaxer or a cold glass of pinot grigio couldn't fix). Ultimately, I worked so hard to create this independent life that I decided I was my own "in case of emergency" contact . . . right? #TotallyRational.

The Latino and I have been dating off and on for more than a year. We broke up and got back together more often than hormonal high school kids. To say our relationship is "complicated" would be generous—it's royally fucked up, six ways from Sunday.

He didn't meet most of my criteria for what I was looking for in a man (see chapter 2)—but he was tall, dark, and handsome . . . and damn near perfect in bed, which always kept me "coming" back for more. But the sex wasn't the only reason I stuck around. I could never put my finger on it, but there was something about him—and us—that excited me. I couldn't walk away. And above all, he was in love with me. It took him more than a year to confess, but I knew it right away.

I've had a long-standing theory that the most successful relationships are those in which the guy loves the woman just a little bit more. It's a widely accepted theory that men cheat more than women because of some innate biological need to "spread their seed." (#Gross. Personally, I think it's their need to spread some whore's legs, but whatever.) However, if a man is in a committed relationship with someone whom he feels is a constant challenge or he considers out of his league, his interest will be held longer and more firmly. #TWSS.

It's the same reason that I have zero interest in the random guy hitting on me at a party, but as soon as I see he's moved on to flirt with some twenty-five-year-old bimbo, I'm eager to get his attention again. It's all sorts of fucked up, but it's life. The same thing goes for the guys; if you decide to get married, make sure he loves you just a little bit more. It's not a surefire way to protect yourself from problems or infidelity, but it can't fucking hurt.

This is what I told myself about the Latino: he was more committed to making our relationship work than I was. Or so I thought. I definitely cared deeply about him, but it wasn't love. To quote my life guru, Carrie Bradshaw, "I'm looking for love. Real love. Ridiculous, inconvenient, consuming, can't-live-without-each-other love."

Did that even exist anymore? Could love be different the second time around? Was I expecting too much? I wasn't sure of anything anymore.

When we first met, he wasn't interested in me, so naturally, that only made me want him more. Yes, we made out in a children's bathroom at my friend Kyle Richards's White Party (#SueMe), but we were torn apart by the hall monitor Lisa Vanderpump before anything good could actually happen—especially if we had a little bit more time and *a lot* more privacy.

Then, poof, the Latino disappeared before we could exchange names, numbers, and clearly any bodily fluids. I knew he worked with Kyle's husband, Mauricio, in the real estate business, so I did a little digging on the company's website, found his e-mail address, and shot him a note:

"Hi. I'm the girl from the bathroom, in case you were wondering."

That was it. #ShortButSweet. I gave Kyle permission to give him my number but *only* if he asked for it. She was *not* allowed to just offer it up! While I was definitely the one pursuing him, I still had to *attempt* to play the game. #KeepItSexy.

The Latino reached out to me a few days later, but it was clear I was some kind of afterthought. He told me he rarely checks the company e-mail, so he gave me his phone number and personal e-mail account. Blah. Blah. Blah.

Like most women, I'm not immune to becoming the "needy girl" (#NotHot), so the more dismissive he was toward me, the more desperate I was for him to pay more attention to me. We started casually spending time together, but it would always be a last-minute invite like "Maybe we can grab dinner later," which usually meant that I was cooking while he watched TV on my couch. It never felt like there was any forethought involved. I was just filling holes in his schedule (or, rather, he was filling mine). Either way, I always jumped at the opportunity to be around him, thereby breaking one of my own *very* important rules in game play. Okay, I was actually breaking two.

First of all, you should never accept a same-day invitation. It usually means that the inviter had other plans that fell through and that you're on the B team. Also, it sort of looks pathetic if you're available on such last-minute notice. Second, don't ever accept a "maybe" invitation. Clearly he's waiting to see if he gets a better offer—and if that happens, you're sitting home alone on your couch while he's out for a fabulous meal with someone he considers a better use of his time than you.

Meanwhile, whenever I tried to make concrete plans with more than a few days' notice, it seemed like every day was occupied by some event:

"Oh, I've got a wedding this weekend."

"Oh, my mom and I have dinner plans that night."

"Oh, I'm going to stay with friends in San Diego."

Spending time getting to know me wasn't a priority for him at all—or so it felt. Welcome to Being the Backup Plan. I was so hungry for his attention that I began doting on him, hoping it would ignite some desire in him to be taken care of. #DoAsISay. #NotAsIDo. If he sent me a text saying, "Work is so crazy . . . I haven't even eaten anything yet," I would show up an hour later with takeout from his favorite lunch place. After the Latino pointed out a $1,000 John Varvatos sweater in a shop window while we were walking down Robertson, I went back, had it wrapped in a big red bow, and gave it to him for his birthday. #ImACatch.

After dating for a few months, we actually made plans (*gasp!*) to spend Halloween together. He scored an invite to my billionaire ex-boyfriend's epic annual haunted house party in Beverly Hills. (The real estate business is a small world in L.A.) After four years of being on the guest list, I figured I was grandfathered in to this epic bash. It was *by far* the best and most exclusive invitation in town—we'd be fools not to go. Plus, my costume was already decided: a slutty *cunt*-ry music singer.

A few days before the party, I texted my billionaire ex-boyfriend that I was looking forward to seeing him that Halloween. A few minutes later, he responded with a message explaining that it would be a good idea if I didn't attend the party this year. Was he fucking kidding me?

"I thought we were friends," I responded. "Why?"

Our breakup was a little rough, but nothing out of the ordinary. We remained close and even saw each other on occasion, so this felt completely out of left field. Had I done something to offend him? Something other than dedicate an entire chapter in my first book to what an amazing man he is? All of my friends were going to be at this party, my children were with their father, and I was going to be the odd woman out.

Apparently his girlfriend (and *now* new baby mama) was uncomfortable with our friendship and preferred I not be in attendance. I found this rationale very odd—especially given that at one point or the other he had dated nearly every other woman who was going to the party. I couldn't help but feel like the little girl in grammar school who was the only one without an invite to the dance. With my ego a bit deflated, I texted the Latino that we would have to find another party, explaining that my ex's new girlfriend didn't want me at this party.

"That sucks," he texted back a few minutes later. "But I sort of already promised my buddy I would take him. Maybe we can meet up after."

Excuse me? Was he seriously going to go to my ex-boyfriend's Halloween party without me? I'm not sure what hurt worse: the fact that he would be at my ex-boyfriend's house surrounded by *every* super-hot chick in Los Angeles strutting around in slutty fucking Halloween costumes, or that he didn't care that I was going to be alone. Both, I decided, equally. (Side note: He went again this year even though I said if he did it would be over. He did, and it isn't.)

When his name started popping up in magazines and blogs shortly after, I began questioning his motives. I kept our relationship very private at first and never publicly spoke about him (until after the show aired), but yet his photo began sprouting up in every single celebrity weekly magazine. The Latino denied up and down that he had any interest in being in the spotlight, but I didn't totally believe it. After all, we did meet while filming *Housewives*. I decided that he was just using me to gain a little bit of attention to help promote his business. But sorry, buddy, this is my life—not an episode of fucking *Million Dollar Listing*. He had a quick appearance on that show also. I sure as hell didn't leak his name to the press or the details of one of our recent dates. This guy was one selfish motherfucker. It was time for a break.

Okay, so I didn't cut him off altogether (did I mention how great he is in bed?), but I began pulling back drastically—and began spending time with other people (enter: the Unicorn Chaser, the Criminal).

Immediately, I felt a change in our dynamic. He began pursuing me. The less interested I seemed, the harder he chased. Maybe he missed the gifts and home-cooked meals . . . or maybe he just missed me. Like my mother says, "Men always remember where they have it best"— especially after you leave their shady fucking asses. I always knew how to play the game, but for some reason I hadn't been playing it with him. Now, the ball was in *my* court.

That's when I switched back to Brandi. As soon as I could feel that he wanted me back, I began punishing him for all the times I felt lonely and used. Why couldn't he just appreciate me from the beginning? But maybe if he did, I wouldn't have been interested. #WhoKnows? I stopped returning his every text and started declining half of his date-night invitations—which now came days, not hours, in advance—with vague responses like, "Sorry. Already have plans. Bummer!"

Eventually he got tired of my icy text responses or would see a photo of me online with another guy, and he quit trying. That's when I would start warming up to him again.

And so goes our exhausting game of cat and mouse. (It's tiring even to write about!) We're together; we're not together. We're fucking; we're not fucking. He's interested; he's not. I'm over it; I'm under him. The smallest remark between us could snowball into World War III at the drop of a dime. I've honestly never bickered with anyone the way I do with the Latino. It's so frequent and erratic that sometimes I even forget where we stand on a given day. Was it passion, or was it just a big old pain in the ass? I've always believed that the person you choose to love should make you a better version of yourself, not a nagging, untrusting bitchy version. #BrandiProblems.

During a particular "on" period, we were spending a lot of time together but *always* ended the night at my house. I knew he had a one-bedroom apartment in Beverly Hills and I didn't care, but he never invited me over. It couldn't be that he was ashamed about his home. Could it? On the few occasions I suggested we stay at his place because it was closer than driving up to Mulholland, the Latino pulled out whatever excuse he could think of:

"I have to work early in the morning. I won't want to wake you."

"My air-conditioning's not working, and it's so hot."

"My place is such a mess."

I have two crazy little boys and two poorly house-trained dogs, but *his* place is a mess? Most days, it looked like a fucking tornado blew right through my family room—and I would catch the Latino scanning the room, resting his eyes on an empty Lunchables box on my coffee table or a pile of wet towels by the back door. I knew he was über-uptight: his hair was impeccably groomed, his Prius was impossibly neat, and even his "comfy" clothes meant a James Perse T-shirt and perfectly tailored jeans. It became obvious he was so embarrassed to show me his home that he decided to overlook the dog hair on my couch. Sure, I had my issues with the Latino, but his rental apartment wasn't one of them.

Living in Los Angeles can *really* fuck with your priorities. He had a really rough breakup with his ex-girlfriend of many years because she left him out of the blue for a very wealthy man. It really did a number on him—and he later confided in me that it was the reason he was so tough on me at first. #MajorTrustIssues. #ICanRelate. At forty-five years old, the Latino created a respectable life for himself—a luxurious life by many people's standards—but there's something about this town that can make you feel like that's not enough. His ex-girlfriend did just that.

I've never been the type of person to care about how much someone is worth or what kind of car they drive. As long as you can afford your life and still pick up the tab for dinner every once in a while, it's none of my fucking business. So I finally demanded to see the Latino's home. We were getting along really well at this point. I had introduced him to the boys as my "real estate agent" (a straight one), and we were talking about taking our first trip together—a weekend getaway to Santa Barbara. If we were going to keep dating, I felt it was important that he show me his home. I wanted to prove to him that it wasn't the size of his bank account that mattered to me—it was the size of his heart, his hands, and, well, you know what else. Plus, I wanted to make sure he wasn't keeping any human fucking heads in his freezer. I've seen enough *Dexter* to recognize the signs. Nine times out of ten, people who were raised as only children and are *that* uptight are serial killers. #Fact. I needed to cover my bases.

The building was one of the more modest on the tree-lined street. We walked the single flight of creaky stairs to the second floor of the building. Once we hit the door to his unit, he was already apologizing for the mess.

There was no mess. It looked like one of those staged apartments that no one actually lives in. It was small and plain, but everything appeared to have a "place," so much so that I didn't even know where to put my purse. I scoured each room for any sign of life and felt relieved when I spotted a small green plant in the kitchen.

Aha, I thought. I could put a check mark next to number four. *He is capable of caring for another living thing.* It wasn't the biggest commitment on earth, but it was better than nothing. Sure, he had been burned in the past, but this was a good sign. All wasn't lost.

I took a few steps closer. *No*, I thought. *It can't be . . . Yes. Yes, it is. It's a fake fucking plant.* Are you kidding me? A fake plant? Honestly, I think I would have preferred finding human body parts in his freezer.

"Dude," I said. "You gotta get rid of that plant."

"Why?" he asked, genuinely shocked. "I've had it for five years!"

"And you'll have it for fifty more; it's not fucking real," I said, disgusted.

"Well, I really like it." He was getting defensive.

"At least get a fucking orchid," I said under my breath, but not soft enough. He looked at me with contempt, so I decided that if I was going to wear the "crazy bitch" hat, I might as well go for it: "Can't you commit to take care of anything?"

We weren't talking about the plant anymore.

"Commit?" the Latino shouted back. He was pissed—and you know what they say about Latin tempers. "Brandi, I'm there whenever you call. You need help looking for a new place? I'm there."

"You get paid for that," I spat back.

By the look in his eyes, this insult clearly stung, but he kept going.

"How about when you have to leave last minute for an injured cousin? I'm there to take care of your dogs and clean your fucking kitchen. I've committed to you. I'm there for you."

"You're only there when the cameras are on!" I yelled. That was my go-to insult for the Latino. For someone who didn't want the spotlight, he always managed to make himself available whenever I was shooting something for the show.

"Right, Brandi," he spat. "And if I'm not there, some other guy is there."

That was his fall-back dagger to hurl my way—my dating other people. I couldn't help if photographers snap pictures of me on dates, I couldn't stop blogs from publishing them, and I sure as hell couldn't stop the Latino from constantly stalking me online. It's not like I was purposefully pushing it down his throat (not always), but we weren't exclusive.

Our fake foliage argument led to yet another break for the Latino and me. In some way the fact that he couldn't even invest in a real fucking plant at forty-five years old was proof to me that I was just wasting my time. And good God, we'd go at each other like rabid dogs—and we always went for the jugular.

Before our epic divorce, I *never* fought like this with my ex-husband. Sure, there were occasional tiffs about the house or boys and perhaps a few bouts of jealousy, but those were the healthy arguments that allow you to grow as a couple. We strolled through our days like fucking Disney characters—and rolled around at night like porn stars. Was love different the second time around? Or maybe I was the one who was different? Or worse, maybe it just wasn't love.

When I met my ex-husband, we had our entire future in front of us, and nothing but time. Now, I'm both blessed and cursed with the wisdom that comes with a failed marriage. I'm no longer that doe-eyed twenty-three-year-old girl (let's be clear, I've always had sort of Asian-y almond-shaped eyes). I wanted the butterflies and the fairy tale that I believed I had before, but maybe that wasn't real. Maybe it was all part of the fantasy. Now, I also wanted a loyal man who could share his life with me and my boys. Was I being unreasonable?

The day my beloved Chica went missing, I was in Palm Springs. My assistant told me frantically that someone had broken into the house. (I always found this suspicious because besides the broken screen in my bathroom, nothing suggested I had been burglarized. The only thing missing was my little brown pup.) Sugar was locked in the office, but Chica was nowhere to be found. I felt paralyzed. I was 250 miles from my house and in the middle of filming for *Housewives*. Was my puppy roaming the streets by herself, or did someone steal her? What if she was sitting in a shelter? She had a weak bladder and couldn't sit in a cage that long. I was having a full-blown panic attack, so I did the first thing that came to mind: I called the Latino. We hadn't spoken since the Battle of the Fake Plant, but I knew he would help me. Even though he couldn't stand that I had potty pads in my family room or that my puppies *had* to sleep in bed with me, he knew how much I loved this dog—and, more importantly, how much Chica loved him.

"I'll go over there," he said. "Calm down, Brandi. I'll go look for her. I promise."

And he did. He told me if I wanted to stay in Palm Springs, he would do whatever he could to find my baby. I was of course already in a car back to Los Angeles, but I appreciated the gesture. The Latino was always there when I needed him most. He spent hours walking around my neighborhood looking for her. He talked to the volunteers at a nearby church and waved down every security guard patrolling the area to give them Chica's description. He traipsed up and down the canyon hiking trails for any sign of my baby. Even though I was freaking the fuck out, I felt just a little better knowing he was looking for her. When day turned into night, he sat in my office calling local shelters and refreshing Craigslist to see if any new postings were put up—and he was still there when my car pulled into the driveway hours later.

He stayed with me that night and held me close, both of us fully clothed, as I cried myself to sleep—and there weren't even any cameras around.

...

Right before I was set to leave for a trip to Puerto Rico
for *Housewives,* the Latino announced that he just *needed* to
talk to me.

"Okay," I said. "Call me."

Minutes later my phone rang.

"Hello," I said, slightly annoyed. I had a lot of shit to do
before my trip! My prescriptions don't fill themselves.

"I think I'm in love with you," he announced.

You could have knocked me over with a fucking feather.
Of course we cared for each other and I knew he loved me,
but I wasn't expecting this kind of declaration.

I was in shock.

"Come to Puerto Rico with me," I blurted out. It was
the only response I could muster. I needed time to process
all of this.

The last man I said "I love you" to is currently living
in a Calabasas mansion with his new wife. Love fucked me
over pretty good the last time around, and I've been running from it for five years now. To be honest, I've always
been a little rough on the Latino for not being the perfect
man. I punished him for not falling for me immediately,
for laughing too hard at his own jokes, and for being a
forty-five-year-old only child who couldn't even invest in a
real fucking plant. After more than a year of "caring
about" each other, he suddenly decided he was "in love"

with me? #WTF! Also, maybe I was becoming super-paranoid (I now constantly keep my curtains closed), but I couldn't help but suspect the timing of his huge proclamation. Just a few days earlier, the gossip websites and magazines had started picking up on rumors that I was dating a former NFL player. Was the Latino jealous? Was he just trying to mark me as his territory? Listen, I'm kinky in the bedroom, but nobody is allowed to piss on me. No "golden showers"—except for maybe in the shower. #Shhh.

"I really can't afford the trip right now, Brandi," he said. I could hear the disappointment in his voice, but he couldn't possibly think I was going to say "I love you" back.

"It's all expenses paid," I chirped, hoping this would persuade him. The line was silent, so I tried a joke: "We're filming it for the show, so you can show off that beach body of yours."

"Honestly, I have a ton of work to do," he finally replied.

What was his fucking problem? If you're in love with a girl and she invites you on a free, tropical getaway, you go, right? But catching up on work is more important? He insisted that he was so backed up with paperwork that taking even three days off would force him way behind where he needed to be before "the end of the quarter." #Whatever.

We talked every day leading up to my trip, and I kept pouting because he wouldn't come. Of course I wanted him there, but I also didn't want yet again to be the single girl on a "romantic" trip with these ladies and their husbands.

I found it odd that I didn't hear from him the day I left for Puerto Rico. By the time I landed on this beautiful island, I was starting to really miss him. Sure, I had been on a few dates with the NFL player, but it wasn't anything serious. The Latino was my *real* boyfriend; we just never talked about being exclusive—and definitely never said the "L" word. Do you even have those conversations at forty? What do you say, "Will you be my girlfriend?" and hand some chick your varsity jacket?

On my second night there I got a three-page text message from the Latino explaining that he just needed to get out of Los Angeles for a while, so he booked a last-minute trip to Italy by himself. Was I losing my mind? Didn't he just tell me he couldn't come with me to Puerto Rico because he couldn't afford it (even though it was free) and he had too much work to do? *Fuck me,* I thought. I was being punished. *Fucking liar,* I thought.

I couldn't figure out if I was actually in love with the Latino or if I just wanted him to love me. Was I so scarred by my past that I sabotaged anything that could be real?

I spent half the trip just stewing over this. The more I thought about it, the more pissed I got. A guy who plans out his weekly wardrobe every Sunday night doesn't just hop a fucking plane to Italy. And it's Italy! It's my favorite place on the planet, and he was going there . . . without me. He had to be lying to me. That's why he said no to Puerto Rico. This trip had been planned all along. But then . . . why did he tell me he was in love with me? I was so confused.

"Excuse me," I said to a flight attendant. "Can I get a glass of wine?" I began mentally rehearsing the verbal beating he would get later.

The Latino finally called two days later from Rome. He was in great spirits, so I considered it my duty to ruin his day—just a little bit. After all, I had been obsessing over this for the past forty-eight hours. I accused him of lying to me, manipulating me, and generally annoying the fuck out of me. In my head, I was convinced he was having a torrid European love affair, but I knew I was just being crazy. Wasn't I?

"You know these phone calls cost five dollars a minute," I said. "For someone who can't afford to take a trip, it's awfully expensive."

He didn't call again.

When he finally returned to Los Angeles, he began texting me again. I had spent the last week telling myself I didn't care if I heard from him, because I'm spending time with a super-hot NFL player.

Only now, his messages were different. It wasn't the same as when he left. They were dismissive and rude. I started to panic. Did I go too far? Was he regretting telling me he loved me? So, I did what any irrational girl would do . . . I decided we needed to talk face-to-face and raced to his apartment without an invite. We hadn't seen each other in ten days—apparently, he extended his week-long vacation. In my heart, I already knew why . . . but I thought maybe if he just saw me again, he'd remember that it was *me* he was in love with.

He answered the door in his "casual" clothes. His skin was sun-kissed, and he looked well rested and relaxed. It pissed me off. I started gunning in on him, giving him the third degree about the trip and every single Facebook status he posted. #MyOwnWorstEnemy. Immediately, his jaw clenched and he became extremely defensive.

"I feel like you met someone else," I yelled. It was the "crazy girl" coming out of me, but his body language and attitude suggested something was off.

"I did," he responded, almost nonchalantly.

I felt the rage bubbling up inside me. My Latino had met someone else.

"Did you sleep with her?" I spat the words at him.

"Yes," he replied, looking directly at me. I felt the tears pooling in my eyes but didn't want to give him the satisfaction of seeing me cry. Of course he was free to have sex with whomever he wanted, but that didn't mean I wanted to actually know about it.

Calmly, I asked if he would tell me what happened.

While in Rome the very first night, he thought it would be fun to crash a nearby wedding. (Seriously, though, what grown-ass man crashes a wedding? Life isn't a fucking Vince Vaughn movie.) He met a thirty-five-year-old brunette woman who had come in from Spain for the nuptials, and they instantly had a connection, he said. Was it necessary to tell me her age? #Asshole. She traveled with *my* Latino for the next nine days up and down the Italian coast.

"Do you have feelings for her?" I asked, numb from this new revelation. I already knew the answer.

"Yes." He looked down at his hands. I knew he didn't want to hurt me.

Looking at him in that moment, I realized something: I was in love with him too just a little bit.

In seven short days, he had fallen in love with another woman. He was so exhausted from our epic tug-of-war that he finally had had enough. It was different from what happened with my ex-husband. In the Latino's eyes, he had opened the door for me to love him back—and I had shut it in his face. He was recovering the only way he knew how—and what we'd been doing for a year and a half. I realized that maybe it was too late for us. I went home and spent that evening crying and pondering love.

I decided to propose to my Latino (kind of).

I drove to his apartment with a huge white orchid in the backseat of my car—it was ridiculous and inconvenient, but all of a sudden the thought of him consumed my every minute. Pulling onto his street, I recognized a strange sensation in my stomach: I had butterflies. But I couldn't chicken out now; I had an important question to ask him: "Would you please be my 'in case of emergency' contact?"

Looking back, I wonder if nowadays I mistake hurt for love. Could it be that the scars of my past have caused me to confuse the two emotions? Why did he deserve my love now after a weeklong fling with someone else? I was torturing myself, but for so long I've been hurting for the men I've loved.

It begs the question: Do I *really* love this man? I'll keep you posted.

Mom's Epilogue

The Real Brandi

Since you have just read this book, I am going to assume that you did so because you enjoyed Brandi's first book so much. Many of you feel you have now "met" Brandi through one media source or another, or perhaps even in person. She is tall, attractive, friendly, mouthy, opinionated, and unfiltered. But you need to know that she is also sensitive, loving, generous to a fault, funny, animated, clever, and bossy. Let me expound even further so you get a better idea of who my daughter is.

Let's start at the beginning. Brandi was born feet first, with the umbilical cord wrapped around her neck three times, and refusing to cry. Her cheeks were pink, her eyes were black, and her head was bald. She was walking at nine months of age, potty-trained herself at age one, and rode a two-wheel bicycle (with no training wheels) at age three and a half. She rarely walked across a room, opting to dance, cartwheel, or somersault instead. Her career aspirations as a child included being a model, or maybe a cashier (she loved cash registers, with all those buttons and automatically opening drawers) or a truck driver. Later it was an actress, a photographer, or a makeup artist. Her favorite colors were pink, purple, and red.

Raising three children is challenging, even when they are the three most amazing children in the world. Yeah, I know, spoken like a true *mom*. When it becomes apparent that one of those children (specifically, Brandi) marches to the beat of an entirely different drummer, you *really* have your work cut out for you. Please don't interpret that as a complaint. I celebrated the fact that Brandi did not always conform to the norms and quite often found myself defending her right to be different.

My children attended parochial school through the eighth grade. Brandi's teachers told me she was very bright. She did struggle some with spelling, but rather than take that as a criticism, I preferred to call it creative spelling (example: "ten-a-shoes" for "tennis shoes"). I wasn't worried . . . I knew she would eventually get it.

When Brandi was in about the third grade, during her actress phase, she so desperately wanted to be in the Christmas pageant that she agreed to play the part of Joseph. The little boy originally cast in the part bowed out because it involved holding Mary's hand, and as we all know, girls have cooties. So Brandi donned a beard and a robe and was father to Baby Jesus. A star was born.

There comes a point in every mother's life when you have to have "the talk" with your children. Mine were still quite young when they benefited from my wisdom on the facts of life. As uncomfortable as it was, I answered their questions as honestly as I could. Imagine my relief when Brandi declared that she thought the whole idea of sexual intercourse was gross and she wasn't ever going to engage in that behavior. Ha! If only!

As I mentioned, Brandi rarely walked anywhere. So the decision was made to enroll her in gymnastics. Brandi's grandmother, who paid for her first year of gymnastics, thought it would be a good way to channel her desire to perform and keep her out of trouble. Yes, she was a talented gymnast but she also had a talent for mischief. During the seven years she was a member of a gymnastics team, she frequently went head-to-head with her coaches and participated in and often instigated her fair share of shenanigans with her teammates. One example that stands out in my mind involved snipping the "tail" off her coach's expensive hairstyle on a dare not only from her teammates but from the woman's husband as well. I offered to reimburse the coach for the price of the do, but she declined. I think she preferred to fume. I never really liked her anyway.

Several of Brandi's antics led to some heated discussions between us. Often, after a disagreement, individuals remain angry and resentful for a while. Some hold on to a grudge forever. Arguments never impacted Brandi the way they do most people. When it was over, it was over. She didn't carry around any resentment or let the arguments burden her. I recall one time when I said something to her, still feeling angry or hurt by an argument we had, and she was surprised at my attitude. After all, the disagreement was ancient history, having taken place at least ten minutes ago. She was so over it and I should be too. Time to move on.

We have all heard that laughter is the best medicine. Brandi had an innate talent for making me laugh. Let's consider for example, the ride to and from her gymnastics training sessions. The drive was at least thirty miles each way and we did that five days a week. Boring! Unless you have a gray curly wig from Halloween, a scarf, and a pair of sunglasses. Then you pretend to be a little old lady hunkered down in the passenger seat of the car, and when someone pulls alongside you, make eye contact, yank off the disguise, and see them react. Hysterical! Then there is the "monkey walk." I can't even describe it except to say . . . thirteen years old, all arms and legs, skinny as a rail, walking like a monkey. Every time she did it I laughed so hard I cried.

Not all of Brandi's career aspirations came to fruition . . . thank goodness. One of her first jobs was as a waitress in the dining room at an assisted-living facility. I think that helped shape her opinion of and respect for the elderly. Although Brandi has affection for and is very protective of the senior citizens in her life, her grandfather (my dad) was her favorite. He had baby fine, soft white hair and a hard-assed attitude. He had retired from the U.S. Army as a master sergeant having served in World War II, the Korean conflict, and the Vietnam War. Many people found him intimidating and/or standoffish. Not Brandi. She saw right through the facade. She instinctively knew that he was a pushover. A little fussing, fawning, and hairstyling and she had him grinning like a Cheshire cat in no time. She spoiled him rotten and he loved it.

Senior citizens aren't her only weakness. Her love for animals is also undeniable. She always has to have pets. Right now she has two yappy little Chihuahuas she rescued from an animal shelter. They are not even close to being perfectly behaved, but she wouldn't trade them for the world. Once, when she was at the veterinarian's office, a young lady, a stranger to Brandi, was crying because she could not afford to have her beloved dog treated, which meant it would likely die. Brandi just whipped out her checkbook and wrote a check. She could not stand the idea of someone losing her pet. She has had many pets, including an orphaned duckling and a praying mantis, and she knows how devastating it is when you lose them. Her Jack Russell terrier was attacked and killed by coyotes, and another dog was lost when a screen was cut during what was thought to be an attempted burglary on her home.

Brandi loves deeply and is generous to a fault. She would give you the shirt off her back if she thought you needed it more than she did (except that she is a skinny bitch and it probably wouldn't fit you anyway). I have witnessed her love and generosity as well as experienced it firsthand. When her world turned upside down in 2009, I worried . . . because she had given so much of herself to her marriage and I was not sure she could find herself again. The fact that Brandi managed not just to survive but to re-create herself has made me proud and provided me with a great sense of relief. She has overcome obstacles—like no credit history and limited liquid assets, which made leasing a car and renting a house extremely humbling experiences. After those were handled, and the realization set in that money could be in short supply due to circumstances beyond her control, it became obvious that earning her own money had to be the next step. Tabloid magazines and TV shows were interested in her side of "the story" and were willing to pay her for it.

Once her name and face became familiar thanks to the media, a fan base began to build . . . especially among the community of mothers and women scorned. They applauded when Brandi didn't just shrivel up and die. I did too! Some critics felt that she should take the Jennifer Aniston (who happens to have plenty of her own $$$$) approach and be quiet. Guess what Brandi would tell them to do? You've heard her say it many times on *RHOBH*. As her mom, I initially found it hard to deal with some of the hurtful things people said about her on gossipy blogs and websites. But I have learned to deal with them my own way. I picture them as unemployed losers who sit around in their pajamas, stuffing their faces with unhealthy food, making nasty comments about people they don't know, and playing computer games all day when they should just focus on getting a life and/or a job. Thinking of her critics in this way is liberating!

I know this must seem a bit sugarcoated, I admit. But trust me, no one is perfect. We have all had our share of moments that we wish we could do over or forget, of which we are not particularly proud. Brandi is a headliner in that category. But you have probably figured that out for yourself, especially if you read her first book.

So, here we are, four and a half years from the time when her life was turned upside down, her heart ripped out and stomped on, her family destroyed, her address changed, and her finances left in a questionable state, and my girl is doing quite well, thank you very much. Although her career defies definition, she is earning her own way in her own way. I would not have expected any less. She has provided a nice home for herself and her sons (not to mention her annoying dogs). When she needs help, she has a close circle of family and friends she can rely on. She welcomes new challenges. She is opinionated and outspoken. She recently told me that she will never, ever depend on a man for money again. She will live her life without apologies and always facing forward. She hopes to fall madly in love again. She is strong, she is invincible, she is woman (thank you, Helen Reddy), and she is my brown-eyed girl (thank you, Van Morrison). I am proud to be her mother.

ACKNOWLEDGMENTS

First and foremost I would like to thank Judy Glanville for being the best mother in the world, and her mother, my Grandma Swinehart, for raising such a spectacular human being. Thank you to my dad for being the best, feistiest dad ever and a wonderful grandpa. Thank you to my big sister, Tricia, and my little brother, Michael, for their amazing ability to hold me up when the chips were down and for encouraging me to write this second book. Thank you to my wonderful agent, Michael Broussard, and my coauthor, Leslie Ann Bruce-Amin—this book wouldn't have been written or even been possible without the two of you. I now count you both as family. Thanks also to Darin Harvey and my agent, Alec Shankman.

My biggest thanks go to my two roommates, also known as my children, Mason and Jake Cibrian. Thank you, boys, for allowing me to use my *own* computer to write this book even though at times it really bugged you both. A special thank-you to Mason, who suggested the cover of my new book be the color yellow (he is always right), and a sweet thank-you to Jake, who, during times of writer's block, could always get me to laugh with his "opera singing." Thank you to all of my amazing friends who have been so supportive and have always jumped to my defense during hard times.

To my editor, Nancy Hancock, who at times could be a very tough cookie but ultimately the hardest working editor I know, thank you for believing in me and riding my ass to get this book finished. Thanks to my publishing team at HarperOne—Suzanne Quist, Janet Evans, Dwight Been, and Suzanne Wickham.

Lastly to my beautiful animals, Sugar, Buddy, and Chica (who is still missing but touches my heart every day), thank you for all the unconditional love.

ABOUT THE AUTHOR

Brandi Glanville is the breakout star of the Bravo reality series *The Real Housewives of Beverly Hills* and author of two *New York Times* bestselling memoirs: *Drinking and Tweeting: And Other Brandi Blunders* and *Drinking and Dating: P.S. Social Media Is Ruining Romance.* The now single mother of two sons has been a pop culture fixture since her very public divorce in 2009; she's appeared in countless weekly magazines (including *People, In Touch Weekly, Life & Style Weekly,* and *Us Weekly*), on entertainment shows (including on *E!, Inside Edition, The View,* and *The Today Show*), and on radio shows (*The Howard Stern Show, Loveline, Playboy,* and more). Glanville has become one of the most "googled" members of Bravo's $500 million Housewives franchise and is currently appearing in the show's fifth season. In her downtime, Glanville enjoys dancing, cooking, golfing, Pilates, hiking, staying active in her charities, and building Lego castles with her boys, Mason and Jake.

Find More Wisdom from the
Real Housewives of Beverly Hills
in Kyle Richards's

Life Is Not a Reality Show

HarperOne
An Imprint of HarperCollins*Publishers*